Word
Wizard

Word
Wizard

Super Bloopers, Rich Reflections,
and Other Acts of Word Magic

Richard Lederer

St. Martin's Griffin
New York

www.stmartins.com

Book design by AMANDA DEWEY

Library of Congress Cataloging-in-Publication Data

Lederer, Richard, 1938–
    Word wizard : super bloopers, rich reflections, and other acts of word magic / Richard Lederer.—1st ed.
        p.   cm.
    ISBN 0-312-35171-2
    EAN 978-0-312-35171-7
    1. English language—Errors of usage—Humor. I. Title.

PN6231.E74L46 2006
428.002'07—dc22

                                                                    2005054417

First Edition: April 2006

10 9 8 7 6 5 4 3 2 1

To my agent, Robin Rue,
for helping me to live the life
that has brought forth this book

Contents

Acknowledgments

Thanks to my publishers for permission to include the following essays and poems in these pages:

Pocket Books/Simon & Schuster: "The Miracle of Language," "In Praise of English," "The Case for Short Words," and "A Man of Fire-New Words" from *The Miracle of Language* (1991); "Sound and Sense," "Beautiful English" (folded into "Sound and Sense"), "English Is a Crazy Language," "The Antics of Semantics," "Janus Words," "Foxen in the Henhice," and "A Uni-Verse of Language" from *Crazy English* (1989); "Cut the Verbal Fat" from *The Write Way* (1995), with Richard Dowis; and "Inky Pinky" from *The Play of Words* (1990).

Wyrick & Company: "The World According to Student

Bloopers" and "Lost in Translation" from *Anguished English* (1987) and "It's a Punderful Life" from *Get Thee to a Punnery* (1988).

Merriam-Webster, Inc.: "Ana Gram, the Juggler," "The Palindromedary," and "A Circus of Poems" from *The Word Circus* (1998).

Oxford University Press: "Weird Words" from my foreword to Erin McKean's *More Weird and Wonderful Words* (2003).

AARP: "The Way We Word" from *AARP TheMagazine* March/April 2005;

St. Martin's Press: "José, Can You See?" and "American History According to Student Bloopers" (folded into "The World According to Student Bloopers") from *The Bride of Anguished English* (2000); "Pun Your Way to Success," "A Declaration of Linguistic Independence," "Stamp Out Fadspeak!" "Writing Is . . . ," "How I Write," and "Confessions of a Verbivore" from *A Man of My Words* (2003); and "On Your Marks!" from *Comma Sense: A Fun-damental Guide to Punctuation* (2005), with John Shore.

Introduction

For more than four decades I've had the joy of writing about language—from puns to punctuation, pronouns to pronunciation, and diction to dictionaries. It's been a hoot—and it just got hootier because my friends at St. Martin's Press have asked me to gather a collection of my best and most popular language pieces into this volume.

They've also asked me to cobble an introduction to each chapter—thirty-four in all—so I'll keep this kickoff to the whole book short.

I appreciate the opportunity to rediscover the delights of these essays and poems and to improve those creations. You can imagine that as the years have rolled by, I have come upon items that I wish I had included in my printed work. Now I get a chance to add to and tinker with my favorite creations. To take just one example, in the original version of "The World According to Student Bloopers," Julius Caesar expires with these immortal words upon his lips: "Tee hee, Brutus!" Years after the publication of that fractured chronicle of the human race, an English teacher in Kansas reported that one of her students had written, "Eat you, Brutus!" in the very same context. I couldn't insert that superior version into the original narrative, but I have made the upgrade in *Word Wizard*.

As an added bonus (but aren't all bonuses added?), a number of the chapters you are about to read have never appeared previously in any of my books.

From the time I began putting my thoughts about words into textbooks and journals, I have always felt that language is the most deeply human of inventions. Words and people are inextricably bound together. Whether the ground of your being is religion or science, you find that language is the hallmark, the defining characteristic that distinguishes humankind from the other creatures that walk and run and crawl and swim and fly in our world.

In the Genesis creation story that so majestically begins the Bible, we note the frequency and importance of verbs of speaking: "And God *said*, Let there be light; and there was light. . . . And God *called* the light Day, and the darkness he *called* Night. . . . And God *said*, Let there be a firmament in the midst of the waters. . . . And God *called* the firmament Heaven." [Emphasis mine.]

Note those verbs of speaking and naming. God doesn't just snap his fingers to bring the things of the universe into existence. He speaks them into being and then names each one. And what happens when God creates Adam?; "And out of the ground the lord God formed every beast of the field, and every fowl of the air; and brought them unto Adam to see what he would call them: and whatsoever Adam called every living creature, that was the name thereof."

In other words, Adam does what God had done: He *names* things. Perhaps this is what the Bible means when it says, "And God said, Let us make man in our own image, after our likeness." Like God, man is a speaker and a namer.

If your mythos is science, you believe that many early hominid species, some of them coexisting, preceded the tenure of *Homo sapiens*. Today we take for granted that we are the only hominid on Earth, yet for at least four million years many hominid species shared the planet, including *Homo habilis*, *Homo erectus*, and, of course, *Homo neanderthalensis*.

What made us different? What allowed us to survive while our precursors disappeared? The answer is on the tip of our tongues. While some of these other species possessed the physical apparatus for speech, only with *Homo sapiens* did speech tremble into birth.

The birth of language is the dawn of humanity, and each is as old as the other. The appearance of language made us human, and our humanity ensured the survival of language. We human beings have always had language because before we had it we were not fully human and the sounds that escaped from the holes in hominid faces were not fully language. Not only do we possess language; we *are* language.

RICHARD LEDERER
San Diego, California
richard.lederer@pobox.com

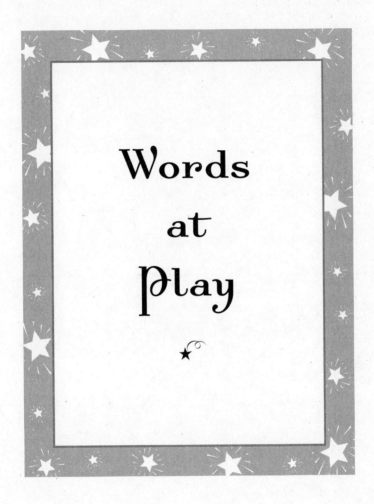

Words
at
Play

In the blunderful world of bloopers, crimes and misdemeanors against the English language go unpunished, but not unpublished, often in my Anguished English series. Although my name appears on the covers of those books, I am not truly their author. My anthologies of accidental assaults upon our language are really created by legions of bloopists who fabricate wacky words, lacerated lingo, ridiculous rhetoric, ditzy diction, fractured phrases, eviscerated expressions, idiotic idioms, mislocated modifiers, mixed-up metaphors, skewed and skewered syntax, and other verbal vagaries. None of these unwitting contributors is a relative of yours, of course.

Blooper Snooper

Some people are bird-watchers. I watch word-botchers. Over the years I've cobbled together five anthologies of fluffs and flubs, goofs and gaffes, blunders, boo-boos, botches, boners, and bloopers. They're the fuel that runs the motor of my career as a fly-by-the-roof-of-the-mouth, word-struck, word-besotted, word-bethumped language guy.

I adhere firmly to the Blooper Snooper's Code of Ethics—that the collector takes what he or she finds and contrives nothing. My specimens are all genuine, certified, and unretouched. No way could I concoct the vivid headline GRAND-MOTHER OF EIGHT MAKES HOLE IN ONE. No way could I improve the receptionist's voice-mail advice "Please leave a message. The doctors are out of the office or else on the phone and me, too." No way could I come close to matching the student who wrote, "The equator is an imaginary lion that runs around the world forever" or the politician who protested to a reporter, "Your question is much too suppository!" These masterpieces of mangled messages are far funnier than anything I could fabricate from whole cloth, even cloth with a lunatic fringe.

Why do readers so delight in bloopers? One clue may come from the origin of the word itself. *Blooper* first appeared in American English in the mid 1920s as a description of a wounded fly ball looped just past the reach of the infielders. Just as bloopers in baseball can make fielders look like bumbling clowns, verbal bloopers can mortify those who make them. Almost at the same time, the verb *to bloop* began to signify the operating of a radio set to cause it or other sets to emit howls and whistles—perhaps an echo of our reactions to physical or verbal howlers. About a decade later, the nouns *bloop* and *blooper* came to signify pratfalls of the body and tongue.

Thomas Fuller once wrote, "Birds are entangled by their feet and men by their tongues." The humor and appeal of bloopers lie, in part, in our awareness of our vulnerability, especially our tendency to trip over our tongues. It is the very artlessness of linguistic lapses that makes them so endearing and makes us feel superior. We laugh when we see and hear verbal rugs pulled out from under someone else. After all, we would never commit such blunders—or would we?

Just as we thrill when the mighty fall in a stage tragedy, we delight when men and women of lofty stature engage their mouths without first putting their brains in gear. Secretary of Defense Donald Rumsfeld, who was a champion college wrestler, wrestled with this shining piece of philosophy as he analyzed Iraq's cache of weapons of mass destruction: "There are known knowns. These are things that we know we know. There are known unknowns. That is to say, there are things that we know we don't know. But there are also unknown unknowns. There are things we don't know we don't know." California governor Arnold Schwarzenegger recently explained, "I think that gay marriage is something that should be between a man and a woman." Gray Davis, the governor whom Arnold replaced, proclaimed, "My vision is to make the most diverse state on earth, and we have people from every planet on the earth in this state." Ah, how the mighty have fallen—usually on their mouths.

The best bloopers inspire the kind of bisociative thinking we experience with puns. But while plays on words exploit the density of language, any denseness residing in bloopers is accidental. Arizona State University humorologists Donald F. and Aileen Pace Nilsen explain:

Blunders and bloopers are genuinely funny because they involve the reader or listener in mentally drawing together two scripts—the one that was said and the one that was intended. To qualify, the error has to be far enough away from the original to communicate some other meaning yet close enough that the listener or reader can connect it to the unintended meaning.

I am often asked, "Do you spend all day reading newspapers, magazines, essays, and signs?" *Au contraire.* I rely on the kindness of total strangers. Sure, I happen to happen on some items myself: A student of mine actually did write, "Romeo's last wish was to be laid by Juliet." But the vast bulk of the rough-and-bumble thud and blunder I publish is sent me by a conspiracy of fellow blooper snoopers from (to mix a metaphor) the four corners of the globe. Just as a certain kind of person walks through a field with eyes peeled for four-leaf clovers, blooper snoopers trek through newspapers, magazines, and books looking for petty crimes and misdemeanors against our language.

Many of these verbal hunter-gatherers wing me mere grammar errors that do not qualify as bloopers: "To be sure, his investments in the media giants wasn't enough to give him editorial control." "Bush knows he can count on Kissinger, who shares he and Dick Cheney's passion for secrecy." The singular form *wasn't* in the first example and the nominative *he* in the second constitute nonstandard usage, but faulty grammar doth not a blooper make. No double entendres (or "double Nintendos," as somebody once blipped) exist here.

I also receive gifts of gaffes that simply aren't funny: "The State Department is understandably loathe to abandon the noble tradition of U.S. leadership in those endeavors." "Following the tenants of both the Zone Diet and the American Heart Association, Balance for Life provides three meals a day plus snacks." In these artifacts we may recognize that *loathe* should be *loath* and *tenants* should be *tenets*, but these inadvertent substitutions do not conjure up any wiggy images that detonate stomachs into a rolling boil.

Every now and then I am granted strings of bright verbal pearls, such as these admissions applications to Bates College in Lewiston, Maine: "I am in the mist of choosing colleges." "I was abducted into the National Honor Society." "I have made the horror role every semester." In many-faceted jewels such as these, we do find a shiny conspiracy of two meanings—one intended and one unwitting—and the conjunction of images sets us to laughter. Of the thousands of specimens of inspired gibberish that I've captured and put on display, my favorite is this gem that gleamed out from a student essay: "Sir Francis Drake circumcised the world with a hundred-foot clipper." The statement is hysterically unhistorical, and we have no trouble believing that a student actually wrote it. How blunderful that one young scholar's innocent malapropizing of *circumnavigate* and accidental pun on *clipper* can beget such nautical naughtiness. This creation is one of the greatest bloopers ever blooped.

A young scholar once wrote, "In 1957, Eugene O'Neill won a Pullet Surprise." One of the fringe benefits of being an English or history teacher is receiving the occasional Pullet Surprise of a student blooper in an essay or answer to a test question.

For Anguished English, my first language book for the larger public, I pasted together the following history of the world from genuine, authentic, certifiable, and unretouched student bloopers collected by teachers around the globe, from eighth grade through college level. Read carefully, and you will learn a lot.

Little did I know at the time that this fractured chronicle of the human race would become the fuel that runs the motor of my career—the riff I am most often requested to perform as a speaker and the progenitor of four additional books in the Anguished English series.

The World According to Student Bloopers

The inhabitants of ancient Egypt were called mummies, and they all wrote in hydraulics. They lived in the Sarah Dessert, which they cultivated by irritation and over which they traveled by Camelot. The climate of the Sarah is such that the inhabitants have to live elsewhere, so certain areas of the dessert are cultivated by irrigation. Ancient Egyptian women wore a calasiris, a loose-fitting garment which started just below the breasts which hung to the floor.

The Bible is full of interesting caricatures. In the first book of the Bible, Guinness, Adam and Eve were created from an apple tree. One of their children, Cain, once asked, "Am I my brother's son?" Noah's wife was called Joan of Ark. Lot's wife was a pillar of salt by day and a ball of fire by night.

God asked Abraham to sacrifice Isaac on Mount Montezuma. Jacob, son of Isaac, stole his brother's birthmark. Jacob was a patriarch, who brought up his twelve sons to be patriarchs, but they did not take to it. One of Jacob's sons, Joseph, gave refuse to the Israelites.

Pharaoh forced the Hebrew slaves to make bread without straw. Moses led them to the Red Sea, where they made unleavened bread, which is bread without any ingredients. Afterward, Moses went up on Mount Cyanide to get the Ten Commandments, but he died before he ever got to Canada. David was a Hebrew king skilled at playing the liar. He fought with the Philatelists, a race of people who lived in Biblical times. Solomon, one of David's sons, had three hundred wives and seven hundred porcupines.

The Greeks were a highly sculptured people, and without them we wouldn't have history. The Greeks invented three kinds of columns—Corinthian, Ironic, and Dork. They also created myths. A myth is a female moth. One myth says that the mother of Achilles dipped him in the river Stynx until he became intolerable. Achilles appears in the *Iliad*, by Homer. Homer also wrote the *Oddity*, in which Penelope was the last hardship that Ulysses endured on his journey. Socrates was a famous Greek teacher who went around giving people advice. They killed him. Socrates died from an overdose of wedlock.

In the Olympic Games, Greeks ran races, jumped, hurled the biscuits, and threw the Java. The reward to the victor was a coral wreath. The government of Athens was democratic because people took the law into their own hands.

Eventually, the Romans came along and conquered the Geeks. History calls people Romans because they never stayed in one place for very long. At Roman banquets, the guests wore garlics in their hair. Julius Caesar extinguished himself on the battlefields of Gaul. The Ides of March murdered him because they thought he was going to be made king. Caesar expired with these immortal words upon his dying lips: "Eat you, Brutus!" Nero was a cruel tyranny who would torture his poor subjects by playing the fiddle to them.

The Romans were overrun by the ball bearings. Then came the Middle Ages, when everyone was middle aged. King Alfred conquered the Dames. King Arthur lived in the age of shivery, with brave knights on prancing horses and beautiful women. King Harold mustarded his troops before the Battle of Hastings. Joan of Arc was burnt to a steak and cannonized by Bernard Shaw. People contracted the blue bonnet plague, which caused them to grow boobs on their necks. Magna Carta provided that no free man should be hanged twice for the same offense. People performed morality plays, about ghosts, goblins, and other mythical creatures.

In midevil times most of the people were alliterate. The greatest writer of the time was Chaucer, who wrote many poems and verses and also wrote literature. Another tale tells of William Tell, who shot an arrow through an apple while standing on his son's head.

The Renaissance was an age in which more individuals felt the value of their human being. Martin Luther was nailed to the church door at Wittenberg for selling papal indulgences. He died a horrible death, being excommunicated by a bull.

It was the sculptor Donatello's interest in the female nude that made him the father of the Renaissance. It was an age of great inventions and discoveries. Gutenberg invented the Bible and removable type. Sir Walter Raleigh discovered cigarettes and started smoking. And Sir Francis Drake circumcised the world with a hundred-foot clipper.

The government of England was a limited mockery. Henry VIII found walking difficult because he had an abbess on his knee. Queen Elizabeth was the Virgin Queen. As a queen she was a success. When Elizabeth exposed herself before her troops, they all shouted, "Hurrah!" Then her navy went out and defeated the Spanish armadillo.

The greatest writer of the Renaissance was William Shakespeare. Shakespeare never made much money and is famous only because of his plays. He lived at Windsor with his merry wives, writing tragedies, comedies, and errors. In one of Shakespeare's famous plays, Hamlet rations out his situation by relieving himself in a long soliloquy. In another, Lady Macbeth tries to convince Macbeth to kill the king by attacking his manhood. Romeo and Juliet are an example of a heroic couplet.

Writing at the same time as Shakespeare was Miguel Cervantes. He wrote *Donkey Hote*. The next great author was John Milton. Milton wrote *Paradise Lost*. Then his wife died, and he wrote *Paradise Regained*.

During the Renaissance America began. Christopher Columbus was a great navigator who discovered America while cursing about the Atlantic. His ships were called the Nina, the Pintacolada, and the Santa Fe. Later the Pilgrims crossed the ocean, and this is known as the Pill's Grim Progress. When they landed at Plymouth Rock, they were greeted by the Indians, who came down the hill rolling their war hoops before them. Many of the Indian heroes were killed along with their cabooses, which proved very fatal to them.

The winter of 1620 was a hard one for the settlers. Many people died and many babies were born. Captain John Smith was responsible for all this.

One of the causes of the Revolutionary War was the English put tacks on their tea. Also, the colonists would send their parcels through the post without stamps. Finally, the colonists won the war and no longer had to pay for taxis.

The United States was founded by four fathers. Delegates from the original thirteen states formed the Contented Congress. Thomas Jefferson, a Virgin, and Benjamin Franklin were two singers of the Declaration of Independence. Franklin had gone to Boston carrying all his clothes in his pocket and a loaf of bread under each arm. He invented electricity by rubbing cats backwards and declared, "A horse divided against itself cannot stand." Franklin died in 1790 and is still dead.

George Washington married Martha Curtis and in due time became the Father of Our Country. Then the Constitution of the United States was adopted to secure domestic hostility. Under the Constitution the people enjoyed the right to keep bare arms.

Abraham Lincoln became America's greatest precedent. Lincoln's mother died in infancy, and he was born in a log cabin which he built with his very own hands. When Lincoln was president, he wore only a tall silk hat. He said, "In onion there is strength." Abraham Lincoln wrote the Gettysburg Address while traveling from Washington to Gettysburg on the back of an envelope.

On the night of April 14, 1865, Lincoln went to the the-ater and got shot in his seat by one of the actors in the moving picture show. The believed assinator was John Wilkes Booth, a supposingly insane actor. This ruined Booth's career.

Meanwhile in Europe, the Enlightenment was a reason-able time. Voltaire invented electricity and also wrote a book called *Candy*. Gravity was invented by Isaac Walton. It is chiefly noticeable in the autumn, when the apples are falling off the trees.

Johann Sebastian Bach wrote a lot of music and had a great many children. He kept an old spinster up in his attic on which he practiced every day. Bach was the most famous composer in the world, and so was Handel. Handel was half-German, half-Italian, and half-English. He was very large. Bach died from 1750 to the present. Ludwig van Beethoven wrote music even though he was deaf. He was so deaf he wrote loud music. He took long walks in the forest even when everyone was calling for him. Beethoven expired in 1827 and later died for this.

France was in a very serious state. The French Revolution was accomplished before it happened. The "Marseillaise" was the theme song of the French Revolution, and it catapulted into Napoleon. During the Napoleonic Wars, the crowned heads of Europe were trembling in their shoes. Then the Spanish gorillas came down from the hills and nipped at Napoleon's flanks. Napoleon became ill with bladder problems and was very tense and unrestrained. He wanted an heir to in-herit his power, but since Josephine was a baroness, she couldn't bear children.

The sun never set on the British Empire because the British Empire is in the East and the sun sets in the West. Queen Victoria was the longest queen. She sat on a thorn for sixty-three years. Her reclining years and finally the end of her life were exemplatory of a great personality. Her death was the final event which ended her reign.

The nineteenth century was a time of many great inventions and thoughts. The invention of the steamboat caused a network of rivers to spring up. Cyrus McCormick invented the McCormick raper, which did the work of a hundred men. Samuel Morse invented a code of telepathy. Louis Pasteur discovered a cure for rabbis. Charles Darwin was a naturalist who wrote the *Organ of the Species*, Madman Curie discovered radio, and Karl Marx became one of the Marx Brothers.

The First World War was caused by the assignation of the Arch-Duck by an anahist. In the Second World War Franklin Roosevelt put a stop to Hitler, who committed suicide in his bunk.

Martin Luther had a dream. He went to Washington and recited his Sermon on the Monument. Later, he nailed ninety-six Protestants in the Watergate Scandal, which ushered in a new error in the anals of human history.

Aside from giving us the kick of hearing someone else screw up, bloopers are entertaining because they reveal hidden connections between words. The potential for bloopers and puns is one of the great joys of our English language, which possesses more than three times the number of words of any other vocabulary. The formula is a simple one: The more words a language owns, the greater the likelihood that collisions will occur and that the witness to such collisions (and in the case of puns, collusions) will explode into laughter.

José, Can You See?

Two men were discussing Beatles songs. "I've never understood," one man wondered, "why they say, 'the girl with colitis goes by.'" After a puzzled pause, his friend lit up. "Ah," he said, "it's 'the girl with kaleidoscope eyes.' That's a line from 'Lucy in the Sky with Diamonds.'"

That's also a classic mondegreen—a mishearing of oft-used

words, resulting in a misinterpretation of the lyrics of popular songs and hymns and the contents of prayers, patriotic affirmations, familiar adages and epigrams, advertising slogans, and the like.

Pop songs yield a bumper crop of mondegreens. "The girl from Emphysema goes walking" is a mondegreen for "the girl from Ipanima goes walking." "The ants are my friends" is a mondegreen for "the answer, my friends, is blowin' in the wind."

"I've thrown a custard in her face" is not the national anthem for clowns. It's a mondegreen for "I've grown accustomed to her face," in My Fair Lady.

"Return December, bad dress unknown" is a mondegreen for "Return to sender, address unknown," and "Don't cry for me, Marge and Tina" a mondegreen for "Don't cry for me, Argentina."

To the surprise of many rock-and-roll enthusiasts, Jimi Hendrix sang, " 'Scuse me while I kiss the sky," not " 'Scuse me while I kiss this guy."

Actually, George Gershwin wrote Rhapsody in Blue, not Rap City in Blue.

"Clown control to Mao Zedong" is at least as colorful and imaginative as David Bowie's original lyric, "Ground control to Major Tom."

Herman's Hermits warbled, "There's a kind of hush all over the world tonight," not "There's a can of fish all over the world tonight." But the fish are better.

And if Davy Crockett was "killed in a bar when he was only three," who was that at the Alamo?

The word *mondegreen* was coined by Sylvia Wright, who wrote about the phenomenon in a 1954 a *Harper's* column, in which she recounted hearing a Scottish folk ballad, "The Bonny Earl of Murray." She heard the lyric "Oh, they have slain the Earl of Murray / And Lady Mondegreen." Wright powerfully identified with Lady Mondegreen, the faithful friend of the Bonny Earl. Lady Mondegreen died for her liege with dignity and tragedy. How romantic!

It was some years later that Sylvia Wright learned that the last two lines of the stanza were really "They have slain the Earl of Murray / And laid him on the green." She named such sweet slips of the ear mondegreens, and thus they have been evermore.

Children are especially prone to fresh and original interpretations of the boundaries that separate words in fresh and unconventional ways. Our patriotic songs and statements have been delightfully revised by misspelt youth:

> *José, can you see*
> *By the Donzerly light?*
> *Oh, the ramrods we washed*
> *Were so gallantly steaming.*
> *And the rockets' red glare,*
> *The bombs bursting in there,*
> *Grapefruit through the night*
> *That our flag was still rare.*

★

I pledge the pigeons to the flag
Of the United States of America
And to the republic for Richard Stans,
One naked individual, underground,
With liver, tea, injustice for all.

★

God bless America, land that I love.
Stand aside, sir, and guide her,
With delight through the light from a bulb.

★

America, America,
God's red Chef Boyardee.

★

Miniza seen the glory
Of the coming of the Lord.
He has trampled out the vintage
Where the great giraffes are stored.

And it's "Oh, beautiful for spacious skies" not "Oh, beautiful for spaceship guys."

Another territory lush with mondegreens is religion. Many a youngster has recited the famous line from the Twenty-third Psalm as "Shirley, good Mrs. Murphy will follow me all the days of my life." Many other imaginary characters inhabit the lyrics of hymns and words from the Bible. Battalions of children have grown up singing about an ophthalmalogically challenged ursine named Gladly—"the cross-eyed bear."

Our Father, Art, in heaven, Harold be Thy name.
Thy King done come, Thy will be done,
On earth as it is in heaven.
Give us this day our jelly bread,
And forgive us our trash passes,
As we forgive those who press past us.
And lead us not into Penn Station,
But deliver us some e-mail.

For religious mondegreens, the fracturing of Christmas carols especially opens up new worlds of meaning and imagination. Try singing along with these new takes on old favorites, revised by children:

- Good King Wences' car backed out
  On a piece of Stephen.
- Deck the halls with Buddy Holly.
- We three kings of porridge and tar
- On the first day of Christmas my tulip gave to me
- Later on we'll perspire, as we dream by the fire.
- He's making a list, of chicken and rice.
- Noel. Noel, Barney's the king of Israel.
- Bells on bobtail ring,
  Making spareribs bright.
- Get a yuck, get a yuck, get a yuck yuck yuck.
- With the jelly toast proclaim
- Olive, the other reindeer
- You'll go down in Listerine.

- Frosty the Snowman is a ferret elf, I say.
- In the meadow we can build a snowman,
  Then pretend that he is sparse and brown.
- Sleep in heavenly peas, sleep in heavenly peas.
- Chipmunks roasting on an open fire.
- Oh, what fun it is to ride with one horse, soap, and hay.
- O come, froggy faithful.
- What a friend we have in cheeses.
- You'll tell Carol, "Be a skunk, I require."
- Where shepherds washed their socks by night
- Get dressed, ye married gentlemen, get huffing you this May.
- Round John Virgin, mother and child,
  Holy Vincent, so tender and mild

I nominate Richard Stans, Art, Harold, good Mrs. Shirley Murphy, Round John Virgin, Vincent, a reindeer named Olive, and that cross-eyed bear named Gladly for a Pullet Surprise. But the ultimate winner, who received her prize posthumorously, of course, must be . . . Lady Mondegreen!

In my anthologies of accidental assaults upon the English language, I've noticed that readers especially enjoy the skewed idioms, bubble-off-plumb word choices, and absurdly literal translations of fractured English abroad. I too chuckle at inspired examples of global gabble, but I always hold in mind a certain serial riddle:

What do you call a person who speaks three languages? Trilingual.

What do you call a person who speaks two languages? Bilingual.

And what do you call a person who speaks one language? American.

In other words, I commend our foreign friends for making the effort at elegant expression in English. I know that their English is a lot better than my Japanese, Chinese, Italian, Spanish, Polish, and German.

Lost in Translation

It is said that someone at the United Nations once fed a common English saying into a translating computer. The machine was asked to translate the statement into Chinese, then into French, and finally back into English.

The adage chosen was "Out of sight, out of mind." What came back was "Invisible insane."

A similar computer was given the task of translating into Russian and then back into English the bromide "The spirit is willing, but the flesh is weak." The result was "The wine is good, but the meat is spoiled."

Why not? "Out of sight" does mean *invisible*, "out of mind" does mean *insane*, *spirit* does mean *wine*, and *flesh* does mean *meat*. Well, sort of. We chuckle at such mechanical renditions, but they remind us that few idioms can be translated word for word from one language to another.

As people around the world have come to recognize and use English as the lingua franca, they have begun adopting our language for the benefit of visitors. Or should I say adapting it, because much of the English abroad is infused with the spirits of Mrs. Malaprop, Samuel Goldwyn, Yogi Berra, Desi Arnaz, Howard Cossell, and Archie Bunker. Consider these examples of outlandish gibberish from hotels around the world:

- *In a Bucharest hotel lobby:* The lift is being fixed for the next day. During that time we regret that you will be unbearable.
- *In a Paris hotel elevator:* Please leave your values at the front desk.
- *In a Yugoslavian hotel:* The flattening of underwear with pleasure is the job of the chambermaid.
- *In a Tokyo hotel:* Is forbitten to steal hotel towels

please. If you are not person to do such thing is please not to read notis.
- *In a Kyoto hotel:* You are invited to take advantage of the chambermaid.
- *In a Tel Aviv hotel:* If you wish for room service breakfast, lift our telephone and the waitress will arrive. This will be enough to bring your food up.

Foreign menus provide a treasure trove of delicious English:

- A Warsaw restaurant exults, "As for the tripe served here, you will be singing its praises to your grandchildren on your deathbed."
- A Swiss menu boasts, "Our wines leave you nothing to hope for."
- A Shanghai Mongolian hot pot buffet guarantees, "You will be able to eat all you wish until you are fed up."
- An Indian restaurant informs us, "Our establishment serves tea in a bag like mother."
- A Chinese menu offers, "Special cocktails for women with nuts."
- A Torremolinas restaurant advises, "We highly recommend the hotel tart."
- An Acapulco restaurant promises, "The manager has personally passed all the water served here."

We venture abroad because we enjoy discovering differences. One of the many pleasures of travel is that of reading and hearing Tinglish, or "tourist English," the developing language of tourism to which postwar air flights have given such a tremendous boost:

- *In a Hong Kong supermarket:* We recommend courteous, efficient self service.
- *In a Bangkok dry cleaner's:* Drop your trousers here for best results.
- *Outside a Paris dress shop:* Dresses for street walking.
- *In a Rhodes tailor shop:* Our your summers suit. Because is big rush we will execute customers in strict rotation.
- *In front of a Madrid travel agency:* Go away.
- *In the Leningrad airport:* This is Leningrad airport and you are welcome to it.
- *In a St. Petersburg, Russia, brochure:* Be sure to visit Senate Square and look at the Copper Horseman, a beautiful erection of Peter the Great.

The Japanese seem to have a special knack for dressing up English in clown suits. These exotic rules of the road are culled from separate signs placed all over Japan:

1. At the rise of the hand of the policeman, stop rapidly. Do not pass him, otherwise disrespect him.

2. When passenger of the foot heave in sight, tootle the horn trumpet melodiously at first. If he still obstacles your passage, tootle with vigor and express by word of mouth the warning "Hai. Hai."

3. Beware of the wandering horse that he shall not take fright as you pass him. Do not explosion the exhaust pipe. Go soothingly by him or stop by the roadside till he pass away.

4. Give big space to the festive dog that make sport in the roadway. Avoid entanglement with your wheel spoke.

5. Go soothingly on the grease mud as there lurk the skid demon.

6. Press the brake of the foot as you roll around the corner to save the collapse and tires up.

The International Tower of Babble is best summarized by signs in Spanish, Mexican, and French shop entrances: "English well talking," "Here speeching American," "Broken English spoken perfectly," and "More or less we speak English." The fact that the speaking an writing of broken English is more than less speeched around the world adds a bit of unscheduled fun to a visit abroad.

Legions of groan-ups think that I'm a compulsive pun-tificator cursed with a puke-ish, not puckish, imagination. They suspect, I suspect, that I'm a member of the Witless Protection Program. That's all right with me because I amused to wit and always bear in mind the slogan of the International Save the Pun Foundation: "A day without puns is a day without sunshine. There is gloom for im-provement." Yes, Virginia, there really is an International Save the Pun Foundation, and yes, they did elect me Inter-national Punster of the Year—the fastest punslinger in the world.

I'm quite serious about the humor of puns, and I hugely enjoyed writing this hymn of praise to the crafty art of punnery.

It's a Punderful Life

Believe it or not, early in January of each year America cele-brates National Save the Pun Week. About this occasion, Dan Carlinsky has observed, "Most folks will probably think that celebrating the pun is about as worthwhile as celebrating a hangnail or a full garbage pail. The pun is the most misun-derstood and most beset-upon form of humor."

Scoffing at puns is a conditioned reflex, and through the centuries groan-ups have aimed a steady barrage of libel and slander at the practice of punning. Three hundred years ago the playwright and critic John Dennis sneered, "A pun is the lowest form of wit"—a charge that has been butted and re-butted by a mighty line of pundits, punheads, pun gents, and pun-up girls.

Henry Erskine, for example, has protested that if a pun is the lowest form of wit, "it is therefore the foundation of all wit." Oscar Levant has added a tag line: "A pun is the lowest form of humor—when you don't think of it first." John Cros-bie and Bob Davies have responded to Dennis with hot, cross puns: "The pun has been said to be the lowest form of humus—earthy wit that everybody digs," and "If someone complains that punning is the lowest form of humor, you can tell them that poetry is verse."

Samuel Johnson, the self-appointed custodian of the En-glish language, once thundered, "To trifle with the vocabu-lary which is the vehicle of social intercourse is to tamper with the currency of human intelligence. He who would violate the sanctities of the Mother Tongue would invade the recesses of the national till without remorse." If lan-guage is money and language manipulators are thieves, Doctor Johnson was a felon, for to him is attributed the following:

I should be punishéd
For every pun I shed:
Do not leave a puny shred
Of my punnish head!

—thus proving the truth of Joseph Addison's pronounce-
ment "The seeds of Punning are in the minds of all men, and
tho' they may be subdued by Reason, Reflection, and good
sense, they will be very apt to shoot up in the greatest Genius,
that is not broken and cultivated by the rules of Art."

Punning is a rewording experience. The inveterate (not
invertebrate) punster believes that a good pun is like a good
steak—a rare medium well-done. In such a prey on words,
rare, medium, and *well-done* are double entendres, so that six
meanings are crammed into the space ordinarily occupied by
just three. That's why the pun is mightier than the sword, and
often sharper. And these days one is much more likely to run
into a pun than into a sword.

Punnery is largely the trick of compacting two or more
ideas within a single word or expression. Punnery challenges
us to apply the greatest pressure per square syllable of language. Punnery surprises us by flouting the law of nature that
pretends that two things cannot occupy the same space at
the same time. Punnery is an exercise of the mind at being
concise.

That many people groan rather than laugh at puns doesn't
mean that the punnery isn't funnery. If the pun is a good one,

the groan usually signifies a kind of suppressed admiration for the verbal acrobatics on display, and perhaps a hidden envy. Edgar Allan Poe (of all people) pointed out that "of puns it has been said that those most dislike who are least able to utter them."

As Francis Bacon once almost said, without hamming it up, some puns are to be tasted, others to be swallowed, and a few to be chewed and digested. Punnery is guaranteed to whet and (great expectorations!) wet your appetite for wordplay. To those who contend that a pun is the lowest form of wit, I counter with the truism that a bun is indeed the doughiest form of wheat.

I am not a fan of the shaggy-dog story, a long, drawn-out narrative that relates an inconsequential happening and finally arrives at a pointless punch line. My personal punster's credo is that plays on words should be clever, appropriate, and short. That's what I like about the playful—and, I hope, helpful—aphorisms in this piece.

Pun Your Way
to Success

Before you start beefing about my spare ribbing, remember that many a meaty pun has been cooked up as advice on how to succeed in the business of life and the life of business. "Don't be a carbon copy of someone else. Make your own impression," punned French philosopher Voltaire. "Even if you're on the right track, you'll get run over if you just sit there," advised humorist Will Rogers centuries later.

Sharpen your pun cells, and let's get right to wit:

- The only place where success comes before work is in the dictionary.
- The difference between a champ and a chump is *u*.
- Triumph is just *umph* added to *try*.
- Don't assume. It will make an *ass* out of *u* and *me*.
- Hard work is the yeast that raises the dough.
- The best vitamin for making friends is B-1.
- Break a bad habit—drop it.
- Patience is counting down without blasting off.
- Patience requires a lot of wait.
- Minds are like parachutes: They function only when open.
- To keep your mind clean and healthy, change it every once in a while.
- You can have an open mind without having a hole in your head.

"Big shots are only little shots that keep on shooting," observed British writer Christopher Morley. Here are some more punderful maxims that merit a blue ribbin'.

- One thing you can give and still keep is your word.
- A diamond is a chunk of coal that made good under pressure.
- When the going gets tough, the tough get going.
- If the going gets easy, you may be going downhill.

- If you must cry over spilled milk, please try to condense it.
- Don't be afraid to go out on a limb—that's where the fruit is.
- Read the Bible—it will scare the hell out of you.
- The Ten Commandments are not multiple choice.
- Failure is the path of least persistence.
- Life is not so much a matter of position as disposition.
- Of all the things you wear, your expression is the most important.
- If at first you don't succeed, try, try a grin.

"Many people would sooner die than think—and usually they do," lamented British philosopher Bertrand Russell, pun in cheek. Some puns can help us to climb the ladder of success without getting rung out:

- People who never make a mistake never make anything else.
- When you feel yourself turning green with envy, you're ripe to be plucked.
- A smile doesn't cost a cent, but it gains a lot of interest.
- Success is more attitude than aptitude.
- Having a sharp tongue can cut your own throat.
- Learn that the bitter can lead to the better.

- He who throws mud loses ground.
- Hug your kids at home, but belt them in a car.
- Fear is the darkroom where negatives are developed.
- Humans are like steel. When they lose their tempers, they are worthless.
- Don't learn safety rules by accident. Don't be dead to rites.
- There are two finishes for automobiles—lacquer and liquor.
- Learn from the nail. Its head keeps it from going too far.
- He who laughs, lasts.

Even though it's a jungle out there, a real zoo, this collection of beastly puns may help you succeed in a workaday world that depends on survival of the fittest:

- Frogs have it easy. They can eat what bugs them.
- There's nothing in the middle of the road but yellow stripes and dead armadillos.
- Birds have bills too, but they keep on singing.
- Don't be like a lemming. Avoid following the crowd and jumping to conclusions.
- Be like a horse with some horse sense—stable thinking and the ability to say nay.
- Be like a dog biting it tail. Make both ends meet.
- Be like a giraffe. Stick your neck out and reach higher than all the others.

- Be like a beaver. Don't get stumped; just cut things down to size.
- Be like a lion. Live life with pride and grab the lion's share with might and main.
- Be like an owl. Be wise but still give a hoot.
- Be like a duck. Keep calm and unruffled on the surface, but paddle like crazy underneath.
- Be like the woodpecker. Just keep pecking away until you finish the job. You'll succeed by using your head.

The
Loom of
Language

People sometimes ask me when I'm going to write the Great American Novel. I tell them, "Never" because long ago I discovered that I stink at creating characters, plots, dialogue, and setting—what Cleanth Brooks has called the "hum and buzz of life." Long ago I discovered that I am primarily an essayist—a communicator of ideas. Ideas are the heroes of my writing; I conjure stories and poems only in the service of those ideas. What fun for me, in the essay that follows, to be able to fashion some honest-to-goodness narrative about the lives of four amazing human beings, each empowered by language.

The Miracle of Language

anguage is the Rubicon that divides man from beast," declared the philologist Max Müller. The boundary between human and animal—between the most primitive savage and the highest ape—is the language line. In some tribes in Africa, a baby is called a *kuntu*, a "thing," not yet a *muntu*, a "person."

It is only through the gift of language that the child acquires reason—the complexity of thought that sets him or her apart from the other creatures who share this planet. The birth of language is the dawn of humanity; in our beginning was the word.

"The limits of my language," wrote the philosopher Ludwig Wittgenstein, "are the limits of my mind. All I know is what I have words for." Without the word we are imprisoned; possessing the word, we are set free. Listen now to the stories of four thinkers—two men, two women; two whites, two blacks—as they give eloquent testimony to the emancipating power of language.

Most of us cannot remember learning our first word, but Helen Keller recalled that event in her life with a flashing vividness. She remembered because she was deaf, mute, and blind from the age of nineteen months and did not learn her first word until she was seven.

When Helen was six, an extraordinary teacher named Anne Mansfield Sullivan entered her life. Miss Sullivan was poor, ill, and nearly blind herself, but she possessed a tenacious vitality that was to force her pupil's unwilling mind from the dark, silent prison in which it lived: "Before my teacher came to me, I lived in a world that was a no-world. I cannot hope to describe adequately that unconscious yet conscious time of nothingness. I did not know that I knew aught, or that I lived or acted or desired."

In his play *The Miracle Worker*, William Gibson shows us what happened when Anne Sullivan first met Helen's mother:

MRS. KELLER: What will you teach her first?

ANNE SULLIVAN: First, last—and in between, language.

MRS. KELLER: Language.

ANNE SULLIVAN: Language is to the mind more than light is to the eye.

The miracle that Anne Sullivan worked was to give Helen Keller language, for only language could transform a small animal that looked like a child, a *kuntu,* into a human being, a *muntu.* Day after day, month after month, Anne Sullivan spelled words into Helen's hand. Finally, when Helen was seven years old and working with her teacher in the presence of water, she spoke her first word. Years later she described that moment in *The Story of My Life* (1902):

> Somehow the mystery of language was revealed to me. I knew then that "w-a-t-e-r" meant that wonderful cool something that was flowing over my hand. That living word awakened my soul, gave it light, hope, joy, set it free! . . . I left the well-house eager to learn. Everything had a name, and each name gave birth to a new thought.

Not only did Helen Keller learn to speak, write, and understand the English language. She graduated cum laude from Radcliffe College and went on to become a distinguished lecturer and writer. But perhaps the most poignant moment in her life came when, at the age of nine, she was able to say to Anne Sullivan, "I am not dumb now."

Richard Wright spent his childhood in the Jim Crow South—a prison of poverty, fear, and racism. He was born on a farm near Natchez, Mississippi, and when he was five, his sharecropper father deserted the family. Richard, his mother, and his brother had to move from one community to another throughout the South, so that he seldom remained in one school for an entire year. Yet somehow Richard Wright escaped the prison of hunger and hatred to become the most significant black writer in America, the author of *Native Son* (1940) and *Black Boy* (1945), two watershed books in American literature.

In *Black Boy*, Wright's unsparing autobiography, he describes his liberation at the age of eighteen. Because black people were not allowed library privileges, Wright used the card of a friendly white man along with a forged note that said, "Dear Madam: Will you please let this nigger boy have some books by H. L. Mencken?" He obtained a copy of Mencken's *A Book of Prefaces*, and all at once the sun of great literature burst through the window of his prison:

> That night in my rented room, while letting the hot water run over my can of pork and beans in the sink, I opened *A Book of Prefaces* and began to read. I was jarred and shocked by the style, the clear, clean, sweeping sentences. Why did he write like that? And how did one write like that? . . . I stood up, trying to

realize what reality lay behind the meaning of the words. . . . Yes, this man was fighting, fighting with words. He was using words as a weapon, using them as one would use a club. . . . Then, maybe, perhaps, I could use them as a weapon? . . .

But what strange world was this? I concluded the book with the conviction that I had somehow over-looked something terribly important in life. I had once tried to write, had once reveled in feeling, had let my crude imagination roam, but the impulse to dream had been slowly beaten out of me by experi-ence. Now it surged up again and I hungered for books, new ways of looking and seeing.

The titles of his first three works—*Uncle Tom's Children*, *Native Son*, and *Black Boy*—keep alive the abiding memory that Richard Wright always carried of the child who opened a book by H. L. Mencken and discovered a world, of the son who never felt himself native to the country of his birth, and of the boy who struggled out of the depths to speak for those who remained behind.

In *The Autobiography of Malcolm X* (1964), Malcolm tells how he rose from a world of thieving, pimping, and drug ped-dling to become one of the most articulate and dynamic leaders of the black revolution in America. Like Helen Keller and Richard Wright, Malcolm X was walled within a prison, in this instance the Norfolk Prison Colony, and, again like them, it was through the gift of language that he gained his liberation.

Frustrated by his inability to express himself in writing, Malcolm borrowed a dictionary from the prison school and slowly, painstakingly, began to copy, word by word and page by page, the entire dictionary onto his tablet: "With every succeeding page, I also learned of people and places and events from history. Actually the dictionary is like a miniature encyclopedia." As his vocabulary expanded, an already-powerful speaker experienced a new empowerment through literacy. He read all day and even at night, in the faint glow of a corridor light:

> Anyone who has read a great deal can imagine the new world that opened up. Let me tell you something: from then until I left that prison, in every free moment I had, if I was not reading in the library, I was reading in my bunk. You couldn't have gotten me out of books with a wedge. . . . Months passed without my even thinking about being imprisoned. In fact, up to then, I had never been so truly free in my life.

The last of our four prisoners is Anne Frank, a young Jewish girl who grew up in Amsterdam during the Nazi occupation of Holland. In July of 1942 Anne's family was forced into hiding in the upper story of an Amsterdam warehouse, where they remained for twenty-five months. The rooms became more suffocating than any prison one could imagine. The Franks, who shared the space with another family and with an elderly dentist, were unable to feel the sun's warmth, unable to breathe fresh air. While the warehouse was in operation during the day, there could be no noise of any kind—no speaking, no unnecessary movements, no running of water.

Then, in 1944, the hideout was discovered by the police. Of the eight who had been crowded into the sealed-off attic rooms, only Mr. Frank survived the ensuing horrors of the concentration camps. In March 1945, two months before the liberation of Holland and three months before her sixteenth birthday, Anne Frank perished in the camp at Bergen-Belsen. According to one witness, she "died peacefully, feeling that nothing bad was happening to her."

Anne may have been devoured by the concentration camps, but her voice was not stilled. From the pages of a small, red-checkered, cloth-covered diary book, she speaks to us across the years. The diary was the favorite gift that Anne received for her thirteenth birthday. She named it Kitty and determined to express to her new confidante her innermost thoughts, concerns, and desires. Between the covers of Kitty the young girl, Anne Frank, recorded her moving commentary on war and its impact on human beings:

> I see the eight of us with our "Secret Annexe" as if we were a little piece of blue heaven, surrounded by heavy black rain clouds. The round, clearly defined spot where we stand is still safe, but the clouds gather more closely about us and the circle which separates us from the approaching danger closes more and more

tightly. Now we are so surrounded by danger and darkness that we bump against each other, as we search
desperately for a means of escape. We all look down
below, where people are fighting each other, we look
above, where it is quiet and beautiful, and meanwhile
we are cut off by the great dark mass, which will not
let us go upwards, but which stands before us as an im-
penetrable wall; it tries to crush us, but cannot do so
yet. I can only cry and implore: "Oh, if only the black
circle could recede and open the way for us!"

Finally the Franks were betrayed, and on August 4, 1944,
the fury of the Gestapo burst upon them. The invaders confis-
cated the silverware and Chanukah candlestick, but they
threw the family's papers to the floor, including Anne's diary,
which was recovered a year later by Mr. Frank.

The Nazis had failed in their mission. *Anne Frank: The
Diary of a Young Girl* was first published in 1947 and has
since been translated into tens of languages and sold millions of copies. No one has described its impact more elo-
quently than Anne's biographer, Ernst Schnabel: "Her voice
was preserved out of the millions that were silenced, this
voice no louder than a child's whisper. . . . It has outlasted
the shouts of the murderers and soared above the voices of
time."

What do the stories of Helen Keller, Richard Wright,
Malcolm X, and Anne Frank say to us? They tell us that the
world we perceive is the world we see through words. They tell

us that, as Wittgenstein once wrote, "of what we cannot speak, we must be silent." They tell us that human beings grapple with the mystery of life by trying to find words to say what it is. They tell us that we must never take for granted the miracle of language.

The twelfth-century chronicler Henry of Huntington observed that an interest in the past is one of the distinguishing characteristics of humankind. The history of the medium through which we communicate our thoughts, passions, and dreams; conduct our business; organize our government; and shape our science, art, and poetry is surely worth studying.

Here, then, is a brief, but I hope exhilarating, tour through the language in which you and I live and move and have our being. In the next chapter we'll journey back together into the history of our American tongue.

In Praise of English

I n the year 1599, the poet and historian Samuel Daniel sang of the English language that was coming to full flower during the Elizabethan Age:

> *And who, in time, knows whither we may vent*
> *The treasure of our tongue, to what strange shores*
> *This gaine of our best glory shall be sent*

T'inrich unknowing Nations with our stores?
What words in the yet unformed Occident
May come refined with the accents that are ours?

The answer to Samuel Daniel's questions is that English, "the treasure of our tongue," has been transported around the globe and has become the most widely spoken language in the history of humankind, the linguistic wonder of the modern world.

The Académie française has announced, with typical Gallic precision, that there are 2,796 languages existing today. Of these, only 10 are the native tongue of more than a 100 million people. Chinese boasts more than a billion native speakers, English 350 million, and then, according to Charles Berlitz in *Native Tongues,* in descending order come Hindustani, Russian, Spanish, Japanese, German, Indonesian, Portuguese, and French.

Although Chinese surpasses English in the sheer number of its native speakers, it does not rival English as a global language. One may legitimately ask if Chinese is indeed a single language as it is subdivided into five distinct dialects that are not mutually intelligible in their spoken forms. While Chinese is largely concentrated in its populous homeland and ethnic enclaves, English is spoken all over the planet by people of all races and nearly all religions and cultures. In fact, recent surveys indicate that those using English as their preferred second language outnumber those who use it natively.

English is the first or official language of forty-five countries covering one-fifth of the earth's land surface. More than 10 percent of the populations of other countries, such as India, Pakistan, Malaysia, Switzerland, Holland, Denmark, and Sweden, are able to converse in English. One out of every seven people in the world—about a billion people—understands and speaks the English language in some form.

The majority of the world's books, newspapers, and magazines are written in English. Most international telephone calls are made in English. Sixty percent of the world's radio programs are beamed in English, and more than 70 percent of international mail and 75 percent of cable messages and telexes are written and addressed in English. It is the language in which two-thirds of all scientific treatises and technical periodicals are printed and 80 percent of all computer text is stored.

The rise of English as a planetary language is an unparalleled success story that begins long ago, in the middle of the fifth century A.D. At the onset of the Dark Ages, several large tribes of sea rovers, the Angles, Saxons, and Jutes, lived along the Continental North Sea coast, from Denmark to Holland. They were a fierce warrior people who built beaked galleys and fought with huge battle-axes and battle hammers, burning towns and carrying off anything they happened to want. Around A.D. 449, these Teutonic plunderers sailed across the water and invaded the islands then known as Britannia. They found the land pleasant and the people, fighting among themselves, very easy to conquer, and so they remained there. They brought with them a Low Germanic tongue that, in its new setting, became Anglo-Saxon, or Old English, the ancestor of the English we use today. During the reign of King Egbert in the ninth century, the land became known as *Englaland*, "the land of the Angles," and the language as *Englisc*, because the Angles were at that time the chief group.

A dramatic evolution in the language came after yet another conquest of England, this one by the Norman French two centuries after the rule of Egbert. The new conquerors came from Normandy, a province of France on the other side of the English Channel. These people had been Vikings and freebooters from the Scandinavian countries who spoke French and had taken to French customs. Their *trouvères*, or minstrels, sang the *Song of Roland* and the legends of the earlier Frankish king Charlemagne.

In 1066, under William, duke of Normandy, the Normans invaded England. In a bloody battle at Hastings, they conquered the Saxons and Danes who resisted them, killed the Saxon king Harold, and forced the nobles to choose Duke William as king of England. One would quite naturally suppose that the language of England would thus come to be French, with only a sprinkling of Anglo-Saxon, but almost the opposite happened. As the invaders, far outnumbered by their captives, lost their ties to France, they took to English as easily as their Norman forebears had dropped their Norse speech for French. Many of their French words entered the vocabulary of their adopted tongue, and the changing language evolved into a form we now call Middle English.

Meanwhile, Latin words had been creeping into the language for many centuries, beginning with the Roman conquest of England in the first century B.C. by Julius Caesar and the influence of the Roman church and missionaries a few centuries later. But the mightiest infusion of Latin words into the great river of English came after the Norman Conquest, either through Norman French or directly from Latin.

The European Renaissance, from the fourteenth into the seventeenth century, began as educated men and women rediscovered the world of ancient Greece and Rome—a world that had been partly shrouded by the darkness of the Middle Ages. The Renaissance was a love affair with anything classical, including all manner of Latin and Greek words, especially those that could name and describe the new discoveries that were bursting forth in science, medicine, art, literature, and world geography. Because these classical words entered the English language primarily through writing, often scholarly writing, they are the kind that we use formally rather than in everyday conversation.

The result of this mingled history is a distinctive three-tiered vocabulary of Anglo-Saxon, French, and classical synonyms that offer us at least three choices for conveying approximately the same meaning. A sampling of these triplets reveals how we can play the music of English with considerably more than one string at just the register we deem most appropriate:

ANGLO-SAXON	FRENCH	LATIN/GREEK
ask	question	interrogate
dead	deceased	defunct
end	finish	conclude
fair	beautiful	attractive
fear	terror	trepidation
help	aid	assist
rise	mount	ascend

Bequeathing us the common words of everyday life, many of them fashioned from a single syllable, Anglo-Saxon is the foundation of our language. Its directness, brevity, and plainness make us feel more deeply and see things about us more truly. The grandeur, sonority, and courtliness of the French elements lift us to another, more literary level of expression. At the third tier, the precision and learnedness of our Greek and Latin vocabulary arouse our minds to more-complex thinking and the making of fine distinctions. Each of us English speakers reenacts the history of our language as we grow up. We acquire the Anglo-Saxon words so early that we can scarcely remember learning them. As we become adults, we learn the harder, more learned words, which generally derive from French, Greek, and Latin.

During the age of Elizabeth I and Shakespeare, the time when Samuel Daniel wrote his poem, English was the mother tongue of only five to seven million speakers tucked away on a foggy island in Western Europe. One of Daniel's contemporaries noted that the language was "of small reatch, it stretcheth no further than this iland of ours, naie not there over all." English was outstripped by French, German, Spanish, and Italian; today it has almost as many speakers as the four put together. Why is it that English has grown a hundredfold in the space of the four centuries that have intervened since the Renaissance? How is it that English has become such a mighty instrument, the most formidable contender for the honor of world tongue?

The emergence of England and then the United States as economic, military, and scientific superpowers has, of course, contributed to the phenomenal spread of the English language. But the essential reasons for the ascendancy of English lie in the internationality of its words and the relative simplicity of its grammar and syntax.

It is often said that what most immediately sets English apart from other languages is the richness of its vocabulary. *Webster's Third New International Dictionary* lists 450,000 words, and the compendious *Oxford English Dictionary* lists 615,000, but that is only part of the total. Technical and scientific terms, family words, slang and argot, and spanking-new creations, unenshrined in ordinary dictionaries, would add hundreds of thousands more, bringing the total of entries to as high as 2 million. In comparison, German, according to traditional estimates, has a vocabulary of about 185,000 words, Russian 130,000, and French fewer than 100,000.

One reason English has accumulated such a vast word hoard is that it is the most hospitable and democratic language that has ever existed. English has never rejected a word because of its race, creed, or national origin. Having welcomed into its vocabulary words from a multitude of other languages and dialects, ancient and modern, far and near, English is unique in the number and variety of its borrowed words. Fewer than 30 percent of our words spring from the original Anglo-Saxon word stock; the rest are imported. As the poet Carl Sandburg once said, "The English language hasn't got where it is by being pure."

Joseph Bellafiore has described the English language as "the lagoon of nations" because "in it there are hundreds of miscellaneous words floating like ships from foreign ports freighted with messages for us." The three largest of those galleons are Latin (from which we derive the likes of *circus*), Greek (*drama*), and French (*garage*). Although Anglo-Saxon is the foundation of the English language, more than 70 percent of our words have been imported from other lands.

Did you know that you speak three hundred languages? Well, you do because you are reading this book and, therefore, speak English. And if you speak English, you speak three hundred languages. To appreciate how cosmopolitan is the word-bearing fleet docked in the wide lagoon of English, examine the following list of fifty familiar English words, along with the languages from which they descend:

Afrikaans: *aardvark*   Australian: *boomerang*
Algonquian: *moose*   Bantu: *zebra*
Arabic: *alcohol*   Basque: *anchovy*
Araucanian: *poncho*   Bengali: *bungalow*

Cantonese: *typhoon*   Lapp: *tundra*

Carib: *hurricane*   Malagasi: *bantam*

Cree: *Eskimo*   Malay: *ketchup*

Czech: *polka*   Maori: *kiwi*

Dakota: *tepee*   Mexican Indian: *coyote*

Danish: *skill*   Norwegian: *shingle*

Dutch: *boss*   Ojibwa: *wigwam*

Egyptian: *oasis*   Persian: *bazaar*

Finnish: *sauna*   Polish: *mazurka*

German: *kindergarten*   Portuguese: *molasses*

Guarani: *jaguar*   Romany: *pal*

Gullah: *jukebox*   Russian: *vodka*

Haitian Creole: *canoe*   Sanskrit: *sugar*

Hawaiian: *ukulele*   Spanish: *rodeo*

Hebrew: *camel*   Swedish: *smorgasbord*

Hungarian: *saber*   Tagalog: *boondocks*

Icelandic: *whisk*   Tahitian: *tattoo*

Irish: *banshee*   Tibetan: *polo*

Italian: *opera*   Turkish: *jackal*

Japanese: *tycoon*   Welsh: *flannel*

Javanese: *batik*   Yiddish: *kibitzer*

No wonder that Ralph Waldo Emerson waxed ecstatic about "English speech, the sea which receives tributaries from every region under heaven," and that Dorothy Thompson, employing a more prosaic metaphor, referred to "that glorious and imperial mongrel, the English language." With its liberal borrowing policy English is easy to learn because it has a familiar look to speakers of other languages. And, by taking in and completely assimilating so many alien words, English has accumulated the most versatile of all vocabularies. Sir Philip Sidney, the quintessential Elizabethan—at once poet, courtier, and soldier—celebrated this word-wealth: "But for the uttering sweetly and properly the conceite of the minde . . . which is the ende of thought . . . English hath it equally with any other tongue in the world." Sidney saw how the abundance of synonyms and near synonyms in our language offers wondrous possibilities for the precise and complete expression of diverse shadings of meaning.

A recent *New Yorker* cartoon puckishly pointed up this treasure trove. The cartoon's caption read "Roget's Brontosaurus," and pictured was a big dinosaur in whose thought bubble appeared: "large, great, huge, considerable, bulky, voluminous, ample, massive, capacious, spacious, mighty, towering, monstrous . . ." Had there been more room, the artist could have added: "vast, enormous, tremendous, gigantic, weighty, sizable, substantial, lumbering, looming, jumbo, leviathan, mountainous, whopping, ponderous, prodigious, colossal, hulking, hefty, husky, humongous." Such a cartoon would be far less likely to appear in a magazine printed in a language other than English. Books like *Roget's Thesaurus* are foreign to speakers of most foreign languages; given the scope and structure of their vocabularies, they have little need of them.

Writer Michael Arlen calls English "the great Wurlitzer of language, the most perfect all-purpose instrument," but, as elaborate as its keyboard is, it is a relatively easy instrument to learn how to play. English possesses a fairly simple, stripped-down apparatus of grammar unencumbered by complex noun and adjective inflections and gender markers. (When I first wrote this chapter, the French were debating whether the word *microchip* should be masculine or feminine.) People often say to me that English must be a very arduous and intimidating language for foreigners to master. How difficult can it be, I answer, when more than 350 million second-language users have learned to speak and understand it? One of these come-latelies to English, Hungarian-born Stephen Baker, tells in *Writer's Digest* of his love for his adopted language:

> No doubt, English was invented in heaven. It must be the lingua franca of the angels.
>
> No other language is like it. Nothing comes even close to it in sound, eloquence, and just plain common sense—and this from someone who spoke nary a word of it before reaching age twenty-five, save for Coke, OK, and drugstore. . . .
>
> You will be surprised to hear me say this: English is probably among the easiest languages to learn—because grammatically it makes sense. Anyone who tells you it isn't should take a trip around the world and listen to tongues wagging. He'll be happy to come home again.

The great nineteenth-century linguist Jakob Grimm wrote, "In richness, good sense, and terse convenience, no other living language may be put beside English." By "terse convenience" Grimm meant that ours is a strikingly direct and concise tongue. Translate a document from English into French or Spanish or German or Russian, and the translation, if true to the original, will emerge about 25 percent longer. Examine bilingual signs and messages, and you will find that the English half is inevitably more compact. In the bathroom of a Toronto hotel in which I stayed are posted these messages, which I reproduce in their exact form:

CONSERVE
PRECIOUS
ENERGY

CONSERVEZ
CETTE
PRECIEUSE
ENERGIE

You can help conserve an adequate supply of energy for all by turning off TV and lights before leaving your room; and by keeping windows closed when heat or air-conditioning is on.

Vous pouvez aider a assurer à tous des approvision- nements énergétiques suffisants en arrêtant le téléviseur et en éteignant les lampes avant de quitter la pièce; et en gardant les fenêtres bien fermées lorsque le chauffage ou la climatisation est en marche.

A careful count of the number of syllables needed to translate the Gospel According to Mark into various languages indicates that, compared to other tongues, brevity is the soul of English:

English	*29,000*
Teutonic languages (average)	*32,650*
French	*36,500*
Slavic languages (average)	*36,500*
Romance languages (average)	*40,200*
Indo-Iranian languages (average)	*43,100*

Although scientists haven't yet discovered the phenomenon, planet Earth is spinning with "reverse English." The language that was forged from invasion has itself become an invader on a global scale. The very English that through the centuries has imported so many words from so many other languages is today one of the world's most popular exports. Through its contributions to other tongues English is beginning to repay its historical debts and establish a linguistic balance of trade.

Pilots and air controllers in all international airports use English to communicate. English lyrics pervade rock music the world over. India, with almost two hundred different languages, relies on English to unify the country. From Athens to Baghdad, from Finland to Kabul, people stand in long lines to sign up for English classes that are vastly oversubscribed.

In a 1990 *New York Times* article, "English Uber Alles," Enno von Lowenstern, deputy editor of the German newspaper *Die Welt*, demonstrated that he could write an article in

German in which the nouns were almost exclusively English. The piece began:

> Unser Way of Life im Media Business ist hart, da muss man ein tougher Kerl sein. Morgens Warm-up und Stretching, dann ein Teller Corn Flakes und ein Soft Drink oder Darjeeling Tea, dann in das office—und schon Brunch mit den Top-Leuten, Meeting zum Thema: Sollen wir die Zeitung pushen mit Snob Appeal oder auf Low Profile achten?

If you were to read German newspapers, you would recognize English words such as *Scoop, Holiday, Paperbacks, Teenagers, Blue Jeans, Cowboys and Indians, Toasters,* and *Mixers,* as well as the sports terms *Ref, Goalkeeper, Puck, Body Check, Punch,* and *Boxing.*

American words have infiltrated even Russian stores with products like *miksers, tosters, komputers,* and *antifriz,* reflecting the fact that half of all foreign-language classes in the Soviet Union are courses in English. By popular Soviet request, the British Broadcasting Corporation is supplying Moscow Radio with a series of programs emphasizing the essential English vocabulary of a capitalist society. To help Soviet listeners tell a stock from a bond and a bull from a bear, the BBC–Moscow Radio broadcasts encourage familiarity with such words and phrases as *collateral, management buyouts, export guarantees, Let's talk about that over lunch,* and *Do we have a deal?* In 1990, for the first time since Fidel Castro took over Cuba, English was taught in that country's elementary schools. Castro reportedly said about the role of English in Cuban education: "Although we might not like it, it's a universal language, the most widespread—much easier to learn than Russian and more precise above all in technical matters."

Many a Japanese businessman has a *kakuteiru* ("cocktail"), perhaps a *jintonikku* ("gin and tonic"), with his *fantazikku garufurendo* ("fantastic girlfriend"). For a snack later in the evening, the couple might choose to have *aisukurimu* or *yoguruto*. If you're not sure what *aisukurimu* and *yoguruto* are, consider that they come in a variety of flavors, among them *chokoreto*, *banira*, and *sutoroberi*.

Japanese ads, posters, and shopping bags display a wiggy kind of American *Ingurisshu* ("English"): "World Smell in Cup Full," "Imagine Folkloric Sports in Summer," "My Life. My Gas," "Just Fit to You, King Kong." A number of these slogans start with an enthusiastic "Let's," as in "Let's Hiking," and "Let's Sports Violent All Day Long." Adorning Japanese clothing, pencil cases, and stationery are messages that also illustrate with charming absurdity the Japanese fascination with English: "Happy Good Day," "Fancy Pimple," and "Persistent Pursuit of Dainty."

The influx of English, especially American English, is not always welcomed abroad with open mouths. The French, who in 1635 formed the Académie française for the purpose of trying to keep the language pure, have erected seawalls against the flood tide of *la langue du Coca-Cola*, as they call American English. They are battling what they consider to be a gypsy moth infestation of such Americanisms as *le drugstore, skyscraper, weekend, shopping, parking, rafting, fast food, jumbo jet,* and *quick lunch,* all in common usage in France. In 1989 the Pasteur Institute of Paris decided to rename three of its most important scientific journals and publish them in English. The Académie française, composed of forty intellectuals, urged the Pasteur Institute to rescind its decision, which it termed "a demonstration of the unjustified surrender of a part of the French scientific community." The institute hasn't backed down.

The English language continues to be one of the world's great growth industries, adding more than a thousand new words a year to its word store and, since World War II, garnering new speakers at an annual rate of about 2 percent. Over the course of a millennium and a half, it has evolved from the rude tongue of a few isolated Germanic tribes into an international medium of exchange in science, commerce, politics, diplomacy, tourism, literature, and pop culture—the closest thing we have ever had to a global language. If ever our descendants make contact with articulate beings from other planets and other solar systems, English will doubtless start adding and assimilating words from Martian, Saturnian, and Alpha Centaurian and beaming its vocabulary across outer space. Then English will become a truly universal language.

An African-American saying tells us, "If somebody asks where you goin', tell 'em where you been." We learn who we are and where we are going by discovering who we were and whence we came.

As long as there are people, these people will have experiences, and experiences continuously mold language into new forms. The story of a nation's language is always closely related to the history of that nation. That's why we Americans—exuberant, innovative, and always reinventing ourselves—speak American, which is exuberant, innovative, and always reinventing itself.

A Declaration of Linguistic Independence

When in the course of human events, it becomes necessary for a people to improvise new words to catch and crystallize the new realities of a new land; to give birth to a new vocabulary endowed with its creators' irrepressible shapes and textures and flavors; to tell tales taller and funnier than anyone else had ever thought to tell before; to establish a body of literature in a national grain; and to harmonize a raucous chorus of immigrant voices and regional lingoes—then this truth becomes self-evident: that a nation possesses the unalienable right to declare its linguistic independence and to spend its life and liberty in the pursuit of a voice to sing of itself in its own words.

Beginning with the Pilgrims, who struggled with Native American words such as *rahaugcum* and *otchock* and transmuted them into *raccoon* and *woodchuck*, the story of language in America is the story of our Declaration of Linguistic Independence, the separating from its parent of that magnificent upstart we call American English.

John Adams was one of the first to lead the charge for American linguistic autonomy. In 1780, sixteen years before he became president, he called upon Congress to establish an academy for "correcting, improving, and ascertaining the English language." Adams proclaimed:

English is destined to be in the next and succeeding centuries more generally the language of the world than Latin was in the last or French is in the present age. The reason of this is obvious, because the increasing population in America, and their universal connection and correspondence with all nations, will, aided by the influence of England in the world, whether great or small, force their language into general use.

At the time Adams made that prediction, an obscure Connecticut schoolmaster was soon to become a one-man academy of American English. His name, now synonymous with *dictionary*, was Webster. Noah Webster saw the untapped promise of the new republic. He was afire with the conviction that a United States no longer dependent on England politically should also become independent in language. In his *Dissertations on the English Language*, published in 1789, Webster declared linguistic war on the King's English:

> As an independent nation, our honor requires us to have a system of our own, in language as well as government. Great Britain, whose children we are, and whose language we speak, should no longer be our standard; for the taste of her writers is already corrupted, and her language on the decline.

In putting this theory into practice, Noah Webster traveled throughout the East and the South, listening to the speech of American people and taking detailed notes. He included in his dictionaries an array of shiny new American words, among them *applesauce, bullfrog, chowder, handy, hickory, succotash, tomahawk*—and *skunk:* "a quadruped remarkable for its smell." Webster also proudly used quotations by Americans to illustrate and clarify many of his definitions. The likes of Ben Franklin, George Washington, John Jay, and Washington Irving took their places as authorities alongside William Shakespeare, John Milton, and the Bible. In shaping the American language, Webster also taught a new nation a new way to spell. He deleted the *u* from words such as *honour* and *labour* and the *k* from words such as *musick* and *publick*, he reversed the last two letters in words such as *centre* and *theatre*, and he Americanized the spelling of words such as *plough* and *gaol*.

In an 1813 letter, Thomas Jefferson echoed Webster and predicted that the vibrant young nation would need many new words. Certainly so great growing a population," he wrote:

> "spread over such an extent of country, with such a variety of climates, of productions, of arts, must enlarge their language, to make it answer its purpose of expressing all ideas. . . . The new circumstances under which we are placed call for new words, new phrases, and for the transfer of old words to new objects. An American dialect will therefore be formed.

Perhaps no one has celebrated this "American dialect" with more passion and vigor than the poet Walt Whitman:

> The Americans are going to be the most fluent and melodious-voiced people in the world—and the most perfect users of words," he yawped barbarically before the Civil War. "The new world, the new times, the new people, the new vistas need a new tongue according— yes, what is more, they will have such a new tongue— will not be satisfied until it is evolved.

More than a century later, it's debatable whether Americans are "the most fluent and melodious-voiced people in the world," but there is no question that we are still engaged in the American Evolution and that our American parlance is as rollicking and pyrotechnic as ever. Consider our invention, in the past fifty years, of delectables on the order of *couch potato*, *mouse potato* (a couch potato attached to a computer), *digerati*, *dot-commer*, *hottie*, *humongous*, *slam dunk*, *sleazebag*, and *soccer mom*.

From the Age of Queen Anne, the British have thundered against what one of their magazines called "the torrent of barbarous phraseology" that poured from the new republic. The first British broadside launched against an Americanism is recorded in 1744, when an English visitor named Francis Moore referred to the young city of Savannah as standing upon a hill overlooking a river "which they in barbarous English call a bluff."

The British were still beating their breasts over what *The Monthly Mirror* called "the corruptions and barbarisms which are hourly obtaining in the speech of our trans-Atlantic colonies" long after we were colonies. They objected to almost every term that they did not consider Standard English, protesting President Jefferson's use of the verb *belittle*. They expressed shock at the American tendency to employ, in place of *suppose*, the likes of *expect*, *reckon*, *calculate*, and—a special target—*guess*, conveniently overlooking Geoffrey Chaucer's centuries-old "Of twenty yeer of age he was, I gesse."

The acidulous British traveler Mrs. Frances Trollope

scoffed in her *Domestic Manners of the Americans* (1832): "I very seldom, during my whole stay in the country, heard a sentence elegantly turned and correctly pronounced from the lips of an American. There is something either in the expression or the accent that jars the feelings and shocks the taste."

Returning from a tour through the United States later in the nineteenth century, the playwright Oscar Wilde sneered, "We really have everything in common with America nowadays except, of course, language." Wilde's fellow playwright George Bernard Shaw observed, "England and America are two countries separated by a common language." But our homegrown treasure Mark Twain put it all into perspective when he quipped about American English, as compared with British English, "The property has gone into the hands of a joint stock company, and we own the bulk of the shares." Or, as that great observer of the American language H. L. Mencken put it, "When two-thirds of the people who use a certain language decide to call it a freight train instead of a goods train, the first is correct usage, and the second is a dialect."

One of the many things I enjoy about writing is embedding the point I am trying to make in the very style of the essay itself. What follows is probably my best-known example of that joyful strategy. A widely circulated magazine published a condensed version of this piece under the title "The Power of a Single Syllable." I pleaded with the editor that changing my title that way put a ding in the unity of style and content that I had tried to achieve in the original. I lost that battle, but the appearance of this riff in that magazine, which I shall not name, allowed millions of readers to digest the nourishment of my message.

Taking off from a piece of classic Xerography, I'm now going to bloviate polysyllabically and loquaciously about this classic hippopotamomonstrosesquipedalian disquisition:

In promulgating your esoteric cogitations or articulating your superficial sentimentalities and amicable, philosophical, or psychological observations, beware of platitudinous ponderosity. Let your conversation and communications possess a clarified conciseness, a compact comprehensibility, a coalescent consistency, and a concatenated cogency. Eschew all conglomerations of flatulent vapidity, jejune babblement, and asinine affectations.

In other words, never use a big word when a diminutive word will do.

The Case for Short Words

When you speak or write, there is no law that says you have to use big words. Short words are as good as long ones, and short, old words—like *sun* and *grass* and *home*—are best of all. A lot of small words—more than you might think—can meet your needs with a strength, grace, and charm that large words do not have.

Big words can make the way dark for those who read what you write and hear what you say. Small words cast their clear light on big things—night and day, love and hate, war and peace, and life and death. Big words at times seem strange to the eye and the ear and the mind and the heart. Small words are the ones we seem to have known from the time we were born, like the hearth fire that warms the home.

Short words are bright like sparks that glow in the night, prompt like the dawn that greets the day, sharp like the blade of a knife, hot like salt tears that scald the cheek, quick like moths that flit from flame to flame, and terse like the dart and sting of a bee.

Here is a sound rule: Use small, old words where you can. If a long word says just what you want to say, do not fear to use it. But know that our tongue is rich in crisp, brisk, swift, short words. Make them the spine and the heart of what you speak and write. Short words are like fast friends. They will not let you down.

The title of this essay and the four paragraphs that you have just read are wrought entirely of words of one syllable. In setting myself this task, I did not feel especially cabined, cribbed, or confined. In fact, the structure helped me to focus on the power of the message I was trying to put across.

One study shows that twenty words account for 25 percent of all spoken English words, and all twenty are monosyllabic. In order of frequency they are: *I, you, the, a, to, is, it, that, of, and, in, what, he, this, have, do, she, not, on,* and *they*. Other studies indicate that the fifty most common words in written English are each made of a single syllable.

For centuries our finest poets and orators have recognized and employed the power of small words to make a straight point between two minds. A great many of our proverbs punch home their points with pithy monosyllables: "Where there's a will, there's a way," "A stitch in time saves nine," "Spare the rod and spoil the child," "A bird in the hand is worth two in the bush."

Nobody used the short word more skillfully than William Shakespeare, whose dying King Lear laments:

> *And my poor fool is hang'd! No, no, no life!*
> *Why should a dog, a horse, a rat have life,*
> *And thou no breath at all? . . .*

Do you see this? Look on her! Look! Her lips!
Look there, look there!

Shakespeare's contemporaries made the King James Bible a centerpiece of short words: "And God said, Let there be light: and there was light. And God saw the light, that it was good." The descendants of such mighty lines live on in the twentieth century. When asked to explain his policy to parliament, Winston Churchill responded with these ringing monosyllables: "I will say: it is to wage war, by sea, land, and air, with all our might and with all the strength that God can give us." In his "Death of the Hired Man," Robert Frost observes: "Home is the place where, when you have to go there, / They have to take you in." And William H. Johnson uses ten two-letter words to explain his secret of success: "If it is to be, / It is up to me."

You don't have to be a great author, statesman, or philosopher to tap the energy and eloquence of small words. Each winter I asked my ninth-graders at St. Paul's School to write a composition composed entirely of one-syllable words. My students greeted my request with obligatory moans and groans, but when they returned to class with their essays, most felt that, with the pressure to produce high-sounding polysyllables removed, they had created some of their most powerful and luminous prose. Here are submissions from two of my ninth-graders:

What can you say to a boy who has left home? You can say
that he has done wrong, but he does not care. He has left

home so that he will not have to deal with what you say. He wants to go as far as he can. He will do what he wants to do.

This boy does not want to be forced to go to church, to comb his hair, or to be on time. A good time for this boy does not lie in your reach, for what you have he does not want. He dreams of ripped jeans, shirts with no starch, and old socks.

So now this boy is on a bus to a place he dreams of, a place with no rules. This boy now walks a strange street, his long hair blown back by the wind. He wears no coat or tie, just jeans and an old shirt. He hates your world, and he has left it.

Charles Shaffer

★

For a long time we cruised by the coast and at last came to a wide bay past the curve of a hill, at the end of which lay a small town. Our long boat ride at an end, we all stretched and stood up to watch as the boat nosed its way in.

The town climbed up the hill that rose from the shore, a space in front of it left bare for the port. Each house was a clean white with sky blue or gray trim; in front of each one was a small yard, edged by a white stone wall strewn with green vines.

As the town basked in the heat of noon, not a thing stirred in the streets or by the shore. The sun beat down on the sea, the land, and the back of our necks, so that, in spite of the breeze that made the vines sway, we all wished we could hide from the glare in a cool, white house. But, as there was no one to help dock the boat, we had to stand and wait.

At last the head of the crew leaped from the side and strode to a large house on the right. He shoved the door wide, poked his head through the gloom, and roared with a fierce voice. Five or six men came out, and soon the port was loud with the clank of chains and creak of planks as the men caught ropes thrown by the crew, pulled them taut, and tied them to posts. Then they set up a rough plank so we could cross from the deck to the shore. We all made for the large house while the crew watched, glad to be rid of us.

Celia Wren

You too can tap into the vitality and vigor of compact expression. Take a suggestion from the highway department. At the boundaries of your speech and prose place a sign that reads, "Caution: Small Words at Work."

You're about to read the results of the greatest magazine commission of my life. Imagine getting a call from AARP—by far the most widely circulated magazine in the world. Imagine the editor asking you to write an article that remembers the words and phrases from the youth of seniors that have gone missing (the words and phrases, not the seniors) and what their vanishing tells us about our lives. If one of the great joys of being a writer is the opportunity to recapitulate one's life, then this assignment was one of the brightest joys of my life as a writer. Shaping this piece led me to discover so much of what I did not know I knew.

The Way We Word

Back in the olden days we had a lot of moxie. We'd put on our best bib and tucker and straighten up and fly right. Hubba-hubba! We'd cut a rug in some juke joint and then go necking and petting and smooching and spooning and billing and cooing and pitch woo in (depending on when we were making all that whoopee) flivvers, tin lizzies, roadsters, hot rods, and jalopies in some passion pit or lovers' lane. Heavens to Betsy! Gee whillikers! Jumpin' Jehoshaphat! Holy moley! We were in like Flynn and living the life of Riley, and even a regular guy couldn't accuse us of being a knucklehead, a nincompoop, or a pill. Not for all the tea in China!

Back in the olden days life was a real gas, a doozy, a dilly, and a pip; flipsville, endsville, the bee's knees, the cat's whiskers, the cat's meow, and the cat's pajamas; far-out, nifty, neat, groovy, ducky, beautiful, fabulous, super, terrif, sweet, and copacetic. Nowadays life is the max, ace, awesome, bad, sweet, fly, kick-ass, gnarly, rad, dank, word, and phat. Life used to be swell, but when's the last time anything was swell? *Swell* has gone the way of beehives, pageboys, and the D. A. (duck's ass), of spats, knickers, fedoras, poodle skirts, saddle shoes, and pedal pushers. Oh, my aching back. Kilroy was here, but he isn't anymore.

Like Washington Irving's Rip Van Winkle and Kurt Vonnegut's Billy Pilgrim, we have become unstuck in time. We wake up from what surely has been just a short nap, and before we can say, "Bob's your uncle!" or "I'll be a monkey's uncle!" or "This is a fine kettle of fish!", we discover that the words we grew up with, the words that seemed omnipresent as oxygen, have vanished with scarcely a notice from our tongues and our pens and our keyboards. Poof, poof, poof go the words of our youth—the words we've left behind. We blink, and they're gone, evanesced from the landscape and wordscape of our perception, like Mickey Mouse wristwatches, hula hoops, skate keys, candy cigarettes, little wax bottles of colored sugar water, and an organ-grinder's monkey.

Where have all those phrases gone? Long time passing. Where have all those phrases gone? Long time ago: *Pshaw. The milkman did it. Think about the starving Armenians. Bigger than a bread box. Banned in Boston. The very idea! It's your nickel. Don't forget to pull the chain. Knee-high to a grasshopper. Turn-of-the-century. Iron curtain. Domino theory. Third world. Fail-safe. Civil defense. You look like the wreck of the Hesperus. Going like sixty. I'll see you in the funny papers. Don't take any wooden nickels. And awa-a-ay we go!*

Oh, my stars and garters! It turns out there are more of these lost words and expressions than Carter had liver pills.

The world spins faster, and the speed of technical advance can make us dizzy. It wasn't that long ago that, in the course of a typical lifetime, only the cast of characters playing out the human drama changed. Now it seems the text of the play itself is revised every day.

Hail and farewell to rumble seats and running boards. Ice-boxes and Frigidaires. Victrolas and hi-fi's. Fountain pens and inkwells. Party lines. Test patterns. Tennis presses. Slide rules. Manual typewriters. Corrasable Bond. Ditto for Photostats and mimeographs. (Do you, like me, remember that turpentiney smell of the mimeo fluid?)

The inexorable advance of technology shapes our culture and the language that reflects it. We used to watch the tube, but televisions aren't made of tubes anymore, so that figure of speech has disappeared. We used to dial telephone numbers and dial up people and places. Now that almost all of us have converted from rotary to push-button phones, we search for a new verb—"Sorry, I must have pushed the wrong number"; "I think I'll punch up Doris"; "I've got to index-finger the Internal Revenue Service"; *Press M for Murder*—and watch *dial* dying on the vine. With modern radios, can the demise of "don't touch that dial!" be far behind?

How many more years do *hot off the press, hung out to dry, put through the wringer,* and *carbon copy* have, now that we no longer print with hot lead, hang wet clothes on clotheslines, operate wringer washing machines, and copy with carbon? Do any young folks still say, "This is where we came in"? The statement means the action or situation is starting to repeat itself, and it comes from the movies. Today there are so many ways of finding out exactly when a movie begins, but back in the olden days we'd get to the theater at pretty much any time and walk in at random. We might watch the last half of a movie and then some trailers, a newsreel, and cartoons (which the multiplexes don't have anymore) and then the second movie in the double feature and then the beginning of the first movie until the point where we could say, "This is where we came in."

Do I sound like a broken record? Do you think I must have been vaccinated with a phonograph needle? In our high-tech times, these metaphors fade away, like sepia photographs in a family album.

Technology has altered our sense of the size of the world and the things in it. Remember the thrill your family felt owning that six-inch black-and-white rabbit-eared television set (soon to be known as the *boob tube* and *idiot box*)? Keep the lights off. No talking, please!

Today more and more TV screens are upwards of forty inches. We drive bigger cars, live in bigger homes, eat bigger meals, and inhabit bigger bodies. I am six feet, three inches, and I used to be called a *six-footer*. Now the NBA is studded with at least a dozen *seven*-footers, and outstanding female athletes, such as Lisa Leslie, Lindsay Davenport, and Venus Williams, regularly and majestically top six feet, so *six-footer* has lost its magic.

How to respond to the supersizing of America? That's the $64 question. The $64 question was the highest award in the 1940s radio quiz show *Take It or Leave it*. By the 1950s, inflation had set in, and $64 no longer seemed wondrous. Then in 1955 came *The $64,000 Question*. The popularity of the show helped *the $64,000 question* become a metaphor for a question whose answer could solve all our problems, but the expression has faded from our lives because that once-sumptuous figure no longer impresses us. Neither does *millionaire* command our awe anymore, now that there are more than two million millionaires in the United States.

While our bodies and our possessions have expanded, our world has grown smaller, and the language of distance has changed. Remember that admonition *Shhh. I'm on long distance!*? Phrases like *long distance* and *coast to coast* and even *worldwide* used to hold such excitement for us. Now we take them for granted, so we hardly ever use them.

Nor do we use the likes of *mailman, fireman, waiter,* and *workman's compensation*. As a culture we have fashioned *letter carrier, firefighter, server,* and *worker's compensation*—genderless terms that avoid setting males as the norm and females as aberrations from that norm.

When's the last time you heard or uttered the word *stewardess*? Now those women and (increasingly) men who try to make us comfortable as we hurtle through the air packed in a winged sardine can have transmogrified into flight attendants. Isn't it wonderful to live in an age when a flight attendant can make a pilot pregnant?

This degendering of our language reflects the new realities of our lives and a growing respect for the humanity of women. Remember *housewife* and *homemaker*? Now we call such a woman *a stay-at-home mom*, respecting her choice to fill such a crucial role. Remember how we used to taunt other kids with "Your mother wears combat [or army] boots!"? These days, your mother could very well be wearing combat boots!

And we've grown more sensitive about other areas of life. Whither *spinsters* and *old maids*, *divorcees*, *illegitimate children*, *juvenile delinquents*, *cripples*, *midgets*, and *the deaf and dumb*? Gone, too, are *Bowery bums* and *tramps* and *hobos riding the rails*. They've left the neighborhood and been replaced by *transients* and the *homeless*—kinder, gentler, less judgmental words that recognize that people living on the street and in the woods usually haven't made some sort of lazy choice to be there.

At the same time we're more blunt about a lot of things. Did women get pregnant when I was a lad? Not that I recall. *Pregnant* was a little too graphic for polite company. Women, instead, were *in a family way* or *expecting*. What they were expecting was *a visit from the stork*.

At the high risk of being labeled a geezer, fogy, and cur-
mudgeon, I'll say right here that along with the bluntness of
modern parlance has arisen a certain impoliteness. Has that
simple first-person pronoun *I* been banished? What we're
hearing these days is "Me and Chip like to go to parties that
blow out our eardrums." To those of us who remember the days
when teachers thought it important to pass the torch of correct English to the next generation, "Me and Chip" squeaks
like chalk scraping across the blackboard of our grammatical
sensibility. But "Me and Chip" is also a social atrocity because
it reverses the rule we were taught back in the olden days: always to put ourselves last in a string of nouns and pronouns.
"Me and Chip" literally reflects a me-first culture. I'll stick
with "Chip and I."

As long as I've left the rant-control district, a certain polite acknowledgment from our youth has gone far south. That
statement is "You're welcome." I'm sitting at a table in a
restaurant, and I ask the server for extra lemon with my tea.
He or she returns with those slices, and I say, "Thank you."
How does the server respond? You know, don't you? Not with
"You're welcome," but with "No problem." No problem? I'm
sure I'm not the only one who wants to grab the server by
the collar and hiss, "You're darned right it's no problem. It's
your job!"

During the past century, the English language has added
an average of nine hundred new words a year. As newly
minted words have added to the currency of our language, the
meanings of the words we grew up with have changed under

our eyes and ears. A *hunk* no longer means simply a large lump of something, and *rap* isn't just sixties talk. *Crack* means more than just a small opening, *ice* more than frozen water, and *pot* more than a cooking utensil. A *pocket* isn't just for pants, and a *bar code* is no longer ethics for lawyers or etiquette in a café. A *pound* is no longer just a unit of currency or measurement but also that tipsy tic-tac-toe game that sits above the "3" on your keyboard or below the "9" on your telephone.

Remember when *IBM* was something a two-year-old might say to a parent? The computer, the most deeply striking technology of our lifetimes, has powerfully challenged our sense of so many hitherto-uncomplicated words—*back up, bit, boot, crash, disk, hacker, icon, mail, memory, menu, mouse, scroll, spam, virus,* and *window.*

Of all the words that have undergone a semantic shift this past half century, the one that rattles the most cages and yanks the most chains is *gay.* We grew up with *gay* as an adjective that meant "exuberant, high-spirited," as in the *Gay Nineties* and *gay divorcee.*

In the second half of the twentieth century, *gay* began traveling the linguistic path of specialization, making the same journey as words such as *chauvinism, segregation, comrade,* and *colored.* Shortly after World War II, activists popularized the concept of Gay Liberation—and many heterosexuals have lamented that a perfectly wonderful word has been lost to general usage, wordnapped by the homosexual community.

But as much as heteros believe they need *gay,* the English language needs it more—as a more fulfilling word for the gay community than *homosexual* because it communicates a culture rather than concentrating on sexual orientation. For those who lament the loss of *gay* to general discourse, I recommend that henceforth they be merry.

This can be disturbing stuff, this winking out of the words of our youth—these words that lodge in our heart's deep core. But just as one never steps into the same river twice, one cannot step into the same language twice. Even as one enters, words are swept downstream into the past, forever making a different river. We of a certain age have been blessed to live in changeful times. For a child each new word is like a shiny toy— a toy that has no age. We at the other end of the chronological and language arc have the advantage of remembering that there are words that once did not exist and that there were words that once strutted their hour upon the earthly stage and that now are heard no more, except in our collective memory. It's one of the greatest advantages of aging. We can have archaic and eat it too.

If we agree that all dogs sound pretty much the same, why do English speakers hear the bark of a dog as bow-wow, while the French hear the same bark as gnaf gnaf, Israelis hear it as have-hav, *and Chinese as* wang-wang? *If words are simply echoes of their natural sounds, why do people sneeze* achoo! *in English, but* up-tchee! *in Russian,* wa-hing! *in Indonesian, and* kychnuti! *in Czech? But surely our all-American cereal, Rice Krispies, goes* Snap! Krackle! *and* Pop! *all around the globe. In Germany, the Krispies do indeed* Schapp! Krackle! *and* Popp! *as they take their milk bath. But the sound is represented in Brazil as* Crik! Crak! Crok! *and in Japan as* Pitchie! Patchie! Putchi! *Such paradoxes have not daunted me from cogitating about the relationships between the sounds of words and what they represent.*

Sound and Sense

What do these words have in common: *bash, clash, crash, dash, gash, gnash, hash, lash, mash, slash, smash, thrash,* and *trash?*

"The words all rhyme," you answer.

Right. But can you spot what it is that the thirteen words share in their content?

Faces are bashed, gashed, slashed, and smashed. Cars crash. Hopes are dashed. Enemies clash. Teeth gnash. Beef is hashed. Potatoes are mashed. Rooms are trashed. And prisoners are lashed and thrashed.

Now the pattern becomes clearer. All of these -ash words are verbs that express terrible actions of great violence. Why, over the more than fifteen-hundred-year history of the English language, have speakers seized on the -ash sound cluster to create words that describe mutilation?

Listen closely to the broad a, and you will hear that it sounds like a drawn-out human scream. Now listen closely to the hissing sound of sh, and note that it too takes a long time to expel. The eighteenth-century English poet Alexander Pope once wrote, "The sound must seem an echo of the sense." It appears that the agonizing, hissy, drawn-out sound of -ash is particularly well suited to the sense of violent actions that unfold over seconds, minutes, or even longer periods of time.

The ancient Greek philosophers Pythagoras (whose theorem of the right triangle we confront in geometry classes), Heraclitus, and Plato subscribed to what many now call the Ding-dong Theory of language origin. They believed that the universe is like a great bell and that every object in nature has a special "ring." Strike an object, and out comes a word the sound of which is inherent in the thing itself.

"Balderdash!" you respond, uttering another mutilative *-ash* word. "Such an a priori correspondence between sound and sense can't possibly exist. Only human beings can invent words; syllables can't repose in things themselves." But, keeping an open mind (rather than a hole in the head), consider the evidence for the validity of the Ding-dong Theory of word formation.

Let's start with initial consonant sounds:

The word for *mother* (and *mama* and *mom*) in an astonishing array of languages begins with the letter *m—mater* (Latin), *mère* (French), *madre* (Spanish), *Mutter* (German), *mam* (Welsh), *mat* (Russian), *ma* (Mandarin Chinese), *me* (Vietnamese), *mama* (Swahili), *makuahine* (Hawaiian), and *masake* (Crow Indian). Could it be more than mere coincidence that this pervasive *m* sound for words maternal is made by the pursing of lips in the manner of the suckling babe?

Think of all the words you know that begin with *fl-*. Your list will probably include the likes of *flicker, flutter, flurry, flip, flap, fly, flow, flash, flee, flare, fling, flush, flame, flail,* and *flounce*. Could the fact that the tongue darts forward whenever we form *fl-* in our mouths account for the sense of movement—usually rapid movement—in all of these words?

Why do so many words beginning with *sn-* pertain to the nose: *snot, sneeze, snort, snore, sniff, sniffle, snuff, snuffle, snarl, snivel, snoot, snout, sneer,* and *snicker*? And why are so many other *sn-* words distasteful and unpleasant: *sneak, snide, snob, snitch, snit, snub, snafu, snoop, snipe, snake,* and *snaggletooth*? To appreciate the nasal aggression inherent in *sn-*, form the sound, and note how your nose begins to wrinkle, your nostrils begin to flare, and your lips draw back to expose your threatening canine teeth.

Think for a moment of how forcibly the sound of an initial *b* is expelled as it flies from the lips like a watermelon seed. Then observe how many words beginning with that letter denote either the expulsion of breath—*breathe, blow, blab, blather, bluster, babble, bloviate,* and *blubber*—or the application of force—*batter, blast, bang, bust, bruise, bludgeon, bump, break, butt, beat, bash, bounce,* and *bomb.*

Listen now to the sounds of vowels in the middle of words:

What happens to the pattern of internal vowels in strong, irregular verbs: *sing, sang, sung; ring, rang, rung?* Place your thumb and forefinger on your Adam's apple as you say these words aloud, and you will notice that as the verbs move backwards in time (today I *sing,* yesterday I *sang,* for years I *have sung*), the vowels themselves echo the process by traveling back in the throat.

Consider the short *i* vowel in words like *little, kid, slim, thin, skinny, imp, shrimp, midget, pygmy,* and *piddling.* What do these words have in common? They all denote smallness or slightness. Why? Perhaps because, when we pronounce the short *i,* we tighten our lips together and make our mouths small.

Now that you are opening your ears to sound and sense, consider these questions about a few sounds that come at the ends of words:

Why is it that many words ending with *-ng* echo with metallic resonance: *bong, boing, gong, ping, ring, clang,* and *ding-dong?*

Why is it that the final voiceless stops *p*, *t*, and *k* come at the end of quick-action words, like *pop*, *clip*, *snip*, *snap*, *rap*, *tap*, *slap*, *whip*, *pat*, *cut*, *slit*, *hit*, *dart*, *flit*, *crack*, *click*, *flick*, *smack*, *whack*, *strike*, and *peck*? Robert Browning put this pattern to sensitive use in "Meeting at Night":

> *A tap at the pane, the quick sharp scratch*
> *And blue spurt of a lighted match*

Why are almost all words that end with *-unk* unpleasant in their suggestions: *clunk*, *junk*, *punk*, *drunk*, *dunk*, *skunk*, *stunk*, *flunk*, *bunk*, *lunk*, *funk*, and *gunk*?

Why do so many words ending with *-ush* have to do with water: *flush*, *gush*, *lush*, *mush*, *rush*, *slush*, and (*orange*) *crush*?

Why does the following cluster of *-allow* words convey qualities that indicate a lack of something? A *callow* youth lacks experience, a *fallow* field lacks use, a *sallow* complexion lacks color, and a *shallow* mind lacks depth.

Why do so many words ending in *-ump* suggest a round mass—*clump*, *rump*, *lump*, *bump*, *mumps*, *plump*, *hump*, *slump*, and *chump* (originally a short, thick piece of wood)? No wonder the great wordsmith and creator of children's stories Lewis Carroll named his rotund egghead *Humpty Dumpty*. Now there's a writer who could really hear and feel the sounds of English words!

Mark Twain plunked the following description into the middle of his "Double-Barreled Detective Story." Read the passage, and reflect on the power of beautiful English words:

It was a crisp and spicy morning in early October. The lilacs and laburnums, lit with the glory-fires of autumn, hung burning and flashing in the upper air, a fairy bridge provided by kind Nature for the wingless wild things that have their homes in the tree-tops and would visit together; the larch and the pomegranate flung their purple and yellow flames in brilliant broad splashes along the slanting sweep of the woodland; the sensuous fragrance of innumerable deciduous flowers rose upon the swooning atmosphere; far in the empty sky a solitary esophagus slept upon motionless wing; everywhere brooded stillness, serenity, and the peace of God.

Did the mellifluous lilting of Twain's prose beguile you into overlooking the basic meaninglessness of the passage, including the absurd sleeping esophagus?

More than sixty years ago, a poll was conducted among American writers to ascertain which English words they considered to be the "most beautiful" in the language. In replying to the question, Louis Untermeyer, the poet and critic, wrote, "The most musical words seem to be those containing the letter *l*. I think, offhand, of such words as *violet, lake, laughter, willow, lovely,* and other such *l*impid and *l*iquid syllables."

Dr. Wilfred Funk, a famous tracker of word origins, chose *tranquil, golden, hush, bobolink, thrush, lullaby, chimes, murmuring, luminous, damask, cerulean, melody, marigold, jonquil, oriole, tendril, myrrh, mignonette, gossamer, fawn, dawn, chalice, anemone, mist, oleander, amaryllis, rosemary, camellia, asphodel,* and *halcyon.*

Lowell Thomas selected *home*, Irvin S. Cobb *Chattanooga*, Charles Swain Thomas *melody*, Stephen D. Wise *nobility*, Lew Sarett *vermilion*, Bess Streeter Aldrich *gracious*, Arnold Bennett *pavement*, George Balch Nevin *lovely*, William McFee *harbors of memory*, and Elias Lieberman the one-word refrain from Edgar Allan Poe's "The Raven"— *nevermore*.

I can't resist adding my personal choices for the most luminous lines in English poetry. Try reading them aloud and listening to their music:

> *Brightness falls from the air;*
> *Queens have died young and fair;*
> *Dust hath closed Helen's eye.*
>
> > Thomas Nash

★

> *In Xanadu did Kubla Khan*
> *A stately pleasure dome decree*
>
> > Samuel Taylor Coleridge

★

> *She walks in beauty, like the night,*
> *Of cloudless climes and starry skies*
>
> > Lord Byron

★

> *Charmed magic casements, opening on the foam*
> *Of perilous seas, in faery lands forlorn*
>
> > John Keats

★

The moan of doves in immemorial elms,
And murmuring of innumerable bees.

Alfred, Lord Tennyson

Now that you have read several dozen words that are considered to be the most beautiful in our language, I wonder if
you might answer a question: Is it possible that we find these
words to be lovely just as much for their meanings and associations as for their sounds? Note, for example, that Dr. Funk's
list is filled with birds and flowers. Is *bobolink* really any more
attractive a word than *condor*, aside from its associations? Is
oriole really more beautiful than *starling*, or, for that matter, are
thrush and *hush* any more euphonious than *mush* and *crush*?

Elias Lieberman may find *nevermore* gorgeous to the ear,
but H. L. Mencken once quoted a Chinese boy who was learning the English language as saying that *cellar door* was the most
musical combination of sounds he had ever heard. One also
thinks of the Mexican poet who picked out *cuspidor* as the
most beautiful word in English.

Clearly the impact that words have upon us is baffling.
Sound and meaning work their dual magic upon us in ways
that ear and mind alone cannot always analyze. Consider, for
example, the foreign couple who decided to name their first
daughter with the most beautiful English word they had ever
heard.

They named the child Diarrhea.

The really scary aspect of this essay is that, in my view, it could not have been written (at least not at this length) thirty or more years ago. To be sure, clichés are almost as old as the English language itself—old as the hills, dead as a doornail, and easy as pie and falling off a log. What's new is that we live in a time when the stitching together of vogue phrases—instantly new clichés—has become a major ingredient of our daily discourse.

Stamp Out Fadspeak!

Some people lament that speaking and writing these days are simply a collection of faddish clichés patched together like the sections of prefabricated houses made of ticky-tacky. They see modern communication as a mindless clacking of trendy expressions, many of them from movies and television sitcoms.

Why is English parlance in such a parlous state? Maybe it's because verbal knee-jerkery requires no thought. It's so much easier not to think, isn't it? It's so much easier to cookie-cut the rich dough of the English language. It's so much easier to microwave a frozen dinner than to create a meal from scratch. After all, when we were children, we loved to pull the string on the doll that said the same thing over and over, again and again.

That's what fadspeak is—the unrelenting mix of mimicry and gimmickry. Fadspeak comprises vogue phrases that suddenly appear on everybody's tongues—phrases that launch a thousand lips. Before you can say, "Yada yada yada," these throwaway expressions become instant clichés, perfect for our throwaway society, like paper wedding dresses for throwaway marriages. Fadspeak clichés lead mayfly lives, counting their duration in months instead of decades. They strut and fret their hour upon the stage of pop culture and then are heard no more.

Now, would I, your faithful, deep-pockets, drop-dead-good-looking language columnist, your poster boy for user-friendly writing, ever serve you anything totally bogus like fadspeak? I don't think so. Not a problem. I have zero tolerance for anything that lowers the bar for what makes world-class writing.

Work with me on this. I've been around the block, and I know a thing or two. I know that I wear many hats, but I'm not talking trash here. I'm not the eight-hundred-pound gorilla out to bust your chops. I feel your pain, and I'm your new best friend. At this point in time, I've got you on my radar screen, and I know you da man! Yessss!

Hey, people, this isn't rocket science or brain surgery. Call me crazy, but it's simply a no-brainer—a dropkick and a slam dunk. I, the mother of all language writers, will go to the mat twenty-four-seven for fresh, original language. You know what? I'm my own toughest critic, so I get more bang for the buck when I avoid those new clichés. I want to level the playing field and give something back to the community. Join the club. Do the math. Get used to it. It works for me. Welcome to my world.

So I'm making you an offer you can't refuse. Maybe it's more than you want to know, but I'm never going to slip into those hackneyed, faddish expressions that afflict our precious American language. Having said that, how about we run that one up the flagpole and see who salutes? Sound like a plan? It's a done deal because I've got a full plate and I bring a lot to the table. I come to play, I bring my A-game, and the ball's in your court.

Sheesh. Get over it. Doesn't it yank your chain, push your buttons, and rattle your cage when a writer or speaker puts dynamite language on the back burner? Doesn't it send you on an emotional roller coaster until you crash and burn when they try to put a good face on it? Doesn't fadspeak just blow you out of the water and make you want to scream, "Oh, puh-leeze! In your dreams! Excuuuuse me! It's my way or the highway! Why are you shooting yourself in the foot? You're history! You're toast! You're going down! That's so twentieth-century! Put a sock in it! Don't give up your day job!"?

As for me, I'm like, "Are you the writer from Hell? You are all over the map. You are like a deer caught in the headlights. Lose the attitude, man. You are so-o-o-o busted. Read my lips! Maybe it's a guy thing, but get real! Get an attitude adjustment.

Get with the twenty-first century! Get a life! And while you're at it, why don't you knock yourself out and get a vocabulary?"

Anyhoo, off the top of my head, the bottom line is that fadspeakers and fadwriters—and you know who you are—are so clueless. I am shocked—shocked!—that they just don't suck it up, get up to speed, go the whole nine yards, push the envelope, take it to another level, and think outside the box. All they do is give you that same-old-same-old, been-there-done-that kind of writing, and you can take that to the bank.

Tell me about it. Fadspeakers and fadwriters just play the old tapes again and again, and their ideas just fall through the cracks. They're not playing with a full deck. The light's on, but nobody's home. Elvis has left the building. Ya think? Go figure.

Hel-lo-oh? Earth to clichémeisters. Duuuh. Boooring. What's wrong with this picture? Are we on the same page? Are we having fun yet? Are you having some kind of a bad-hair day? Are you having a midlife crisis? A senior moment? Maybe it's time for a wake-up call? Or maybe a reality check? I don't think so. In your dreams. Not even close.

O-o-k-a-a-y. You wanna talk about it? You wanna get with the program? Why don't you wake up and smell the coffee? How about we cut right to the chase? I mean, what part of "fadspeak" don't you understand? Deal with it. You got that right. Or maybe I'm just preaching to the choir.

Whatever. As if.

Now that I've got your attention, here's the buzz on viable, cutting-edge communication. Whenever I find some of these snippets of fadspeak strewn about a sentence, I'm in your face. I'm your worst nightmare. Those flavor-of-the-month phrases just make me go ballistic, even to the point of going postal. After all—and I'm not making this up—what goes around comes around.

All right. My bad. I understand that you're not a happy camper, and maybe you just don't want to go there. But I do because I've got all my ducks in a row. I mean, at the end of the day, is this a great language—or what? I mean, it's a language to die for. I mean, if they can put a man on the moon, why can't they teach people to write well?

Gimme a break. Cut me some slack. What am I, chopped liver? Hey, what do I know? And now that I've thrown my hissy fit about fadspeak, here's what's going down.

Thanks a bunch for letting me share. Now that I've been able to tell it like it is, it's time to pack it in. I'm outa here. Talk to you soon. Buh-bye—and have a nice day.

Crazy
English

Contrary to what you might think, as a language grows over time and accumulates increasing numbers of speakers, it tends to become simpler. Some of the most complex languages on earth are spoken by small, close-knit populations living in rain forests. The ubiquitous English language, in contrast, is relatively simple, regular, and streamlined. Still, it's fun to focus on the relatively small number of exceptions to the linguistic rules in our tongue.

If plagiarism is the sincerest form of flattery, I am one of the most flattered people alive. Every day my readers out there in cyberspace unknowingly e-mail me my own material, and more often than not, that material is some form of my exploration of crazy English. I'd prefer that my thoughts be accompanied by attribution, of course, but I'm pleased to see that my words about words are shared by so many fellow verbivores.

English Is a Crazy Language

English is the most widely spoken language in the history of our planet, used in some way by at least one out of every seven human beings around the globe. Half of the world's books are written in English, and the majority of international telephone calls are made in English. Sixty percent of the world's radio programs are beamed in English, and more than 70 percent of international mail is written and addressed in English.

English has acquired the largest vocabulary of all the world's languages, perhaps as many as two million words, and has generated one of the noblest bodies of literature in the annals of the human race. Nonetheless, it is now time to face the fact that English is a crazy language—the most loopy and wiggy of all tongues.

In what other language do people drive in a parkway and park in driveway?

In what other language do people play at a recital and recite at a play?

Why does night fall but never break and day break but never fall?

Why is it that when we transport something by car, it's called *a shipment*, but when we transport something by ship, it's called *cargo*?

Why does a man get a *her*nia and a woman a *hyster*ectomy?

Why do we pack suits in a garment bag and garments in a suitcase?

Why do privates eat in the general mess and generals eat in the private mess?

Why do we call it *newsprint* when it contains no printing, but when we put print on it, we call it a *newspaper*?

Why are people who ride motorcycles called *bikers* and people who ride bikes called *cyclists*?

Why—in our crazy language—can your nose run and your feet smell?

Language is like the air we breathe. It's invisible, inescapable, and indispensable, and we take it for granted. But when we take the time to step back and listen to the sounds that escape from the holes in people's faces and to explore the paradoxes and vagaries of English, we find that hot dogs can be cold, darkrooms can be lit, homework can be done in school, nightmares can take place in broad daylight while morning sickness and daydreaming can take place at night, tomboys are girls and midwives can be men, hours—especially happy hours and rush hours—often last longer than sixty minutes, quicksand works *very* slowly, boxing rings are square, silverware and glasses can be made of plastic and tablecloths of paper, most telephones are dialed by being punched (or pushed?), and most bathrooms don't have any baths in them. In fact, a dog can go to the bathroom under a tree—no bath, no room; it's still going to the bathroom. And doesn't it seem a little bizarre that we go to the bathroom in order to go to the bathroom?

Why is it that a woman can man a station but a man can't woman one, that a man can father a movement but a woman can't mother one, and that a king rules a kingdom but a queen doesn't rule a queendom? How did all those Renaissance men reproduce when there don't seem to have been any Renaissance women?

Sometimes you have to believe that all English speakers should be committed to an asylum for the verbally insane:

In what other language do they call the third hand on the clock the second hand?

Why do they call them *apartments* when they're all together?

Why do we call them *buildings* when they're already built?

Why is it called a *TV set* when you get only one?

Why is the person to whom you've entrusted your hard-earned life savings called a *broker*?

Why is the game called *tug-of-war* when it's actually tug-of-rope, and shouldn't tugboats be called *pushboats*?

Why do they call food servers *waiters* when it's the customers who do the waiting?

Why is *phonetic* not spelled phonetically? Why is it so hard to remember how to spell *mnemonic*? Why doesn't *onomatopoeia* sound like what it is? Why is the word *abbreviation* so long? Why is *diminutive* so undiminutive? Why does the word *monosyllabic* consist of five syllables? Why is there no synonym for *synonym* or *thesaurus*? And why, pray tell, does *lisp* have an *s* in it?

English is crazy.

If adults commit adultery, do infants commit infantry? If olive oil is made from olives, what do they make baby oil from? If a vegetarian eats vegetables, what does a humanitarian consume? If a pronoun replaces a noun, does a proverb replace a verb? If *pro* and *con* are opposites, is *congress* the opposite of *progress*?

Why can you call a woman a mouse but not a rat—a kitten but not a cat? Why is it that a woman can be a vision, but not a sight—unless your eyes hurt? Then she can be "a sight for sore eyes."

A writer is someone who writes, and a stinger is something that stings. But fingers don't fing, grocers don't groce, hammers don't ham, humdingers don't humding, ushers don't ush, and haberdashers do not haberdash.

If the plural of *tooth* is *teeth*, shouldn't the plural of *booth* be *beeth*? One goose, two geese—so one moose, two meese? One index, two indices—one Kleenex, two Kleenices? If people ring a bell today and rang a bell yesterday, why don't we say that they flang a ball? If they wrote a letter, perhaps they also bote their tongue. If the teacher taught, why isn't it also true that the preacher praught? Why is it that the sun shone yesterday while I shined my shoes, that I treaded water and then trod on the beach, and that I flew out to see a World Series game in which my favorite player flied out?

If we conceive a conception and receive at a reception, why don't we grieve a greption and believe a beleption? If a firefighter fights fire, what does a freedom fighter fight? If a horsehair mat is made from the hair of horses, from what is a mohair coat made?

A *slim chance* and *a fat chance* are the same, as are *a caregiver* and *a caretaker*, *a bad licking* and *a good licking*, and "What's going on?" and "What's coming off?" But *a wise man* and *a wise guy* are opposites. How can *sharp speech* and *blunt speech* be the same and *quite a lot* and *quite a few* the same, while *overlook* and *oversee* are opposites? How can the weather be *hot as hell* one day and *cold as hell* the next?

If *button* and *unbutton* and *tie* and *untie* are opposites, why are *loosen* and *unloosen* and *ravel* and *unravel* the same? If *bad* is the opposite of *good*, *hard* the opposite of *soft*, and *up* the opposite of *down*, why are *badly* and *goodly*, *hardly* and *softly*, and *upright* and *downright* not opposing pairs? If harmless actions are the opposite of harmful actions, why are shameful behavior and shameless behavior the same and pricey objects less expensive than priceless ones? If appropriate and inappropriate remarks and passable and impassable mountain trails are opposites, why are flammable and inflammable materials, heritable and inheritable property, and passive and impassive people the same? How can valuable objects be less valuable than invaluable ones? If *uplift* is the same as *lift up*, why are *upset* and *set up* opposite in meaning? Why are *pertinent* and *impertinent*, *canny* and *uncanny*, and *famous* and *infamous* neither opposites nor the same? How can *raise* and *raze* and *reckless* and *wreckless* be opposites when the words in each pair contain the same sound?

Why is it that when the sun or the moon or the stars are out, they are visible, but when the lights are out, they are invisible; that when I clip a coupon from a newspaper, I separate it, but when I clip a coupon to a newspaper, I fasten it; and that when I wind up my watch, I start it, but when I wind up this essay, I shall end it?

English is a crazy language.

How can expressions like "I'm mad about my flat," "No football coaches allowed," "I'll come by in the morning and knock you up," and "Keep your pecker up" convey such different messages in two countries that purport to speak the same English?

How can it be easier to assent than to dissent but harder to ascend than to descend? Why is it that a man with hair on his head has more hair than a man with hairs on his head; that if you decide to be bad forever, you choose to be bad for good; and that if you choose to wear only your left shoe, then your left one is right, and your right one is left? Right?

In the rigid expressions that wear tonal grooves in the record of our language, *beck* can appear only with *call*, *cranny* with *nook*, *hue* with *cry*, *main* with *might*, *fettle* only with *fine*, *aback* with *taken*, *caboodle* with *kit*, and *spick* and *span* only with each other. Why must all shrifts be short, all lucre filthy, all bystanders innocent, and all bedfellows strange? I'm convinced that some shrifts are lengthy and that some lucre is squeaky-clean, and I've certainly met guilty bystanders and perfectly normal bedfellows.

Why is it that only swoops are fell? Sure, the verbivorous William Shakespeare invented the expression "one fell swoop," but why can't strokes, swings, acts, and the like also be fell? Why are we allowed to vent our spleens but never our kidneys or livers? Why must it be only our minds that are boggled and never our eyes or our hearts? Why can't eyes and jars be ajar, as well as doors? Why must aspersions always be cast and never hurled or lobbed?

Doesn't it seem just a little wifty that we can make amends but never just one amend; that no matter how carefully we comb through the annals of history, we can never discover just one annal; that we can never pull a shenanigan, be in a doldrum, eat an egg Benedict, or get just one jitter, a willy, a delirium tremen, or a heebie-jeebie? Why, sifting through the wreckage of a disaster, can we never find just one smithereen?

Indeed, this whole business of plurals that don't have matching singulars reminds me to ask this burning question, one that has puzzled scholars for decades: If you have a bunch of odds and ends and you get rid of or sell off all but one of them, what do you call that doohickey with which you're left?

What do you make of the fact that we can talk about certain things and ideas only when they are absent? Once they appear, our blessed English doesn't allow us to describe them. Have you ever seen a horseful carriage or a strapful gown? Have you ever run into someone who was combobulated,

sheveled, gruntled, chalant, plussed, ruly, gainly, maculate, pe-
cunious, or peccable? Have you ever met a sung hero or experienced requited love? I know people who are no spring
chickens, but where, pray tell, are the people who *are* spring
chickens? Where are the people who actually *would* hurt a fly?
All the time I meet people who *are* great shakes, who *can* cut
the mustard, who *can* fight City Hall, who *are* my cup of tea,
who *would* lift a finger to help, who *would* give you the time of
day, and whom I *would* touch with a ten-foot pole, but I can't
talk about them in English—and that *is* a laughing matter.

If the truth be told, all languages are a little crazy. As Walt
Whitman might proclaim, they contradict themselves. That's
because language is invented, not discovered, by boys and girls
and men and women, not computers. As such, language reflects the creative and fearful asymmetry of the human race,
which, of course, isn't really a race at all.

That's why we wear a pair of pants but, except on very
cold days, not a pair of shirts. That's why men wear a bathing
suit and bathing trunks at the same time. That's why *brassiere*
is singular but *panties* is plural.

That's why *six, seven, eight,* and *nine* change to *sixty, sev-
enty, eighty,* and *ninety,* but *two, three, four,* and *five* do not become *twoty, threety, fourty,* and *fivety.* That's why first-degree
murder is more serious than third-degree murder, but a third-
degree burn is more serious than a first-degree burn. That's
why we can open up the floor, climb the walls, raise the roof,
pick up the house, and bring down the house.

You have to marvel at the unique lunacy of the English

language, in which you can turn a light on and you can turn a light off and you can turn a light out, but you can't turn a light in; in which the sun comes up and goes down, but prices go up and come down—a gloriously wiggy tongue in which your house can simultaneously burn up and burn down and your car can slow up and slow down, in which you fill in a form by filling out a form, in which your alarm clock goes off by going on, in which you are inoculated for measles by being inoculated against measles, in which you add up a column of figures by adding them down, and in which you first chop a tree down—and then you chop it up.

Words do not fall from the sky or turn up under trees or rocks. Language is invented, not discovered. When we think about invention, we usually think of creations like the wheel, the electric light, and the automobile—things that humankind has not always possessed. Words are such an integral part of our consciousness that we believe they have always existed, like stones and grass and bushes. But this is not true. Like flint tools and weaving, each new word is a human invention, spoken or written for the very first time by a particular human being at a particular moment. We human beings are the word makers, and it is we who decide what words mean and when their meanings change.

The Antics of
Semantics

Has it ever struck you how human words are?

Like people, words are born, grow up, get married, have children, and even die. They may be very old, like *man* and *wife* and *home*. They may be very young, like *def* and *McJob*. They may be newly born and struggling to live, as *palmtop*, and *cybrarian*. Or they may repose in the tomb of history, as *leechcraft*, the Anglo-Saxon word for the practice of medicine, and *murfles*, a long-defunct word for freckles or pimples.

Our lives are filled with people and words, and in both cases we are bound to be impressed with their vast numbers and infinite variety. Some words, like *OK*, are famous all over the world. Others, like *foozle* ("a bungling golf stroke") and *groak* ("to stare at other people's food, hoping that they will offer you some"), are scarcely known, even at home.

There are some words that we will probably never meet, such as *samara* (pinwheels that grow on maple trees) and *vomer* (the slender bone separating the nostrils), and others that are with us every day of our lives, such as *I, the, and, to,* and *of,* the five most frequently used English words.

As with people, words have all sorts of shapes, sizes, backgrounds, and personalities. They may be very small, like *a* and *I.* They may be very large, like *pneumonoultramicroscopicsilicovolcanoconiosis,* a forty-five-letter hippopotomonstrosesquipedalian word for black lung disease.

Some words are multinational in their heritage, as *remacadamize,* which is Latin, Celtic, Hebrew, and Greek in parentage. Some come of Old English stock, as *sun* and *moon* and *grass* and *goodness.* Some have a distinctly Continental flavor—*kindergarten, lingerie, spaghetti.* Others are unmistakably American—*stunt* and *baseball.*

Words like *remunerative, encomium,* and *perspicacious* are so dignified that they can intimidate us, while others, like *booze, burp,* and *blubber,* are markedly inelegant in character. Some words, such as *ecdysiast,* H. L. Mencken's Greek-derived name for a stripteaser, love to put on fancy airs; others, like *blogosphere* and *palimony,* are winkingly playful. Certain words strike us as beautiful, like *luminous* and *gossamer,* others as rather ugly—*guzzle* and *scrod;* some as quiet—*dawn* and *dusk,* others as noisy—*thunder* and *crash.*

Like people, words grow after they are born; once created, they seldom sit still and remain the same in their meanings. Some words expand and take over larger territories. They begin with a precise meaning, but their boundaries widen and often grow fuzzier and less definite. A fabulous example of this expansive process is the word *fabulous.* Once *fabulous* meant "resembling or based on a fable." Later came the meaning "incredible, marvelous" because fables often contained incredible and marvelous characters and events. These days the word is weakening in meaning even more, and anything can be fabulous: The latest styles of blue jeans are fabulous, as is *Paradise Lost;* the latest breakthroughs in computers are fabulous, and so is the current Picasso exhibit.

A *picture* was once a painted representation of something seen; now any visual representation—photograph, pen and ink, crayon, a movie—is a picture. A *holiday* first signified "a holy day," but modern holidays include secular days off like Valentine's Day and Independence Day. Not only has the *holy* part of the compound generalized, but so has the *day* part.

Thus, a holiday can now last more than twenty-four hours, as in "I'm going on holiday to the Caribbean."

Other words travel in exactly the opposite direction, narrowing to acquire more specific meanings than the ones with which they started life. Once, at the end of a Chinese meal, my daughter Katherine opened a fortune cookie and read this message inside: "You are genial, clever, intellectual, and discriminating." "But," she protested, "I don't discriminate!" My perceptive child was being sensitive to the fact that *discriminate* has taken on the specialized meaning of making choices in matters of race. Much the same thing has happened to the words *segregation, colored, chauvinism, comrade, fairy, queer, queen,* and *gay.* In *Little Women* (1870), Louisa May Alcott wrote without any ambiguity whatsoever, "As Mrs. March would say, what can you do to four gay girls in the house?"

No word is born shrinkproof. The older meaning of *meat* was "food," of *liquor* "drink," and of *corn* "grain." Early in its life, *starve* meant "to perish." A *hound* was originally "a dog," a *foul* "a bird," and a *deer* "any small animal," as used in William Shakespeare's *King Lear:* "But mice and rats and such small deer / Have been Tom's food for seven long year."

Originally the title *doctor* was given to anyone skilled in a learned profession. An *undertaker* once could undertake to do anything; nowadays undertakers specifically manage funerals. Incredibly, a *girl* once could be a boy, as during the Middle English period *girl* was a unisex word denoting any child or youth.

Business started out as a general term meaning literally "busy-ness; one's proper concern." After a couple of centuries of life, *business* picked up the narrower meaning of "commercial dealings." In 1925, Henry Ford used the word in both its generalized and specialized senses when he stated, "The chief business of the American people is business." We today can see the word starting to generalize back to its first meaning in phrases like "I don't like this funny business one bit."

Some words born into low station have come up in life. With the passing of time, certain positions have acquired *prestige* (which used to mean "trickery") and *glamour* (which started out as a synonym for "grammar"), and the words describing those positions have risen from the humble to the exalted. Such are the histories of *knight*, which once meant "a boy," *lord* (loaf giver), *governor* (steersman), *marshal* (house servant), *squire* (shield bearer), *chamberlain* (room attendant), *constable* (stable attendant), *steward* (sty warden), *minister* (servant), and *pedagogue* (slave). In Geoffrey Chaucer's Middle English, *nice*, derived from the Latin *nescius*, "ignorant," meant "foolish, senseless," and in William Shakespeare's day *politician* was a sinister word implying a scheming, Machiavellian trickster. Although some would argue that the second word really hasn't changed very much, these words have come up in life.

For the most part, however, the reputations of words, like those of people, are quite fragile and subject to debasement. An Englishman was served a delicious meal in an American household. Afterward, he complimented his hostess with "You are the homeliest woman I have ever met!" This was high praise in British English, in which *homely* meant and still means "homelike, good around the home." But because it was perceived that women who stayed home were generally unattractive, the word has taken on negative associations in American English. A similar fate has befallen *spinster*, which, as its roots indicate, meant simply "a woman who spins." The Greeks used *idiotes*, from the root *idios*, "private," to designate those who did not hold public office. Because such people possessed no special skill or status, the word gradually fell into disrepute.

Stink and *stench* were formerly neutral in meaning and referred to any smell, as did *reek*, which once had the innocuous meaning of "to smoke, emanate." William Shakespeare wrote his great sonnet sequence just at the time that *reek* was beginning to degrade, and he exploited the double meaning in his whimsical Sonnet CXXX:

> *My mistress' eyes are nothing like the sun,*
> *Coral is far more red than her lips' red.*
> *If snow be white, why then her breasts are dun,*
> *If hair be wires, black wires grow on her head.*
> *I have seen roses damasked, red and white,*
> *But no such roses see I on her cheeks.*
> *But in some perfume there is more delight*
> *Than in the breath that from my mistress reeks.*

Do you find my treatment of changing word meanings to be vulgar, villainous, boorish, notorious, egregious, smug, silly, or Mickey Mouse? The first seven of these adjectives possessed complimentary or neutral meanings during the Middle Ages: *vulgar, villainous,* and *boorish:* relating to the common people, or peasantry; *notorious* and *egregious:* well-known, outstanding; *smug:* neat, trim; *silly:* good, blessed, innocent.

Until the 1940s, when one said, "Mickey Mouse," one meant only the animated all-American rodent who performed heroic deeds and squeaked his undying love for Minnie. Then came World War II and the subsequent flooding of world markets with Mickey Mouse wristwatches. Because these watches were generally cheap affairs, subject to chronic and chronometric mainspring breakdowns, people started associating anything shoddy or trivial with *mickey mouse,* often lowercased, as in "I'm tired of having to do mickey mouse chores."

Is there a human weakness revealed in this tendency to degrade the meanings of words? Would we rather be critical than complimentary? Or is it rather that the most powerful connotations—those that eventually change the denotation of a word—are the unpleasant ones?

From a creature who is a little lower than the angels and a little higher than the apes, who embraces tiger and lamb, Apollo and Dionysus, the Oedipus Cycle and the Three Stooges, we can expect nothing more or less than an outpouring of words that are brightly rational, surprisingly serviceable, maddeningly random, frenetically creative, and as mutable and mercurial as our very lives.

You've just seen how words can expand or contract or go up or down in life. Some of our words wander so wondrously that they can travel in opposite directions at the same time. Members of this category provide powerful testimony that language reflects the unpredictable and contradictory nature of the people who make it. As Walt Whitman sang, "Do I contradict myself? Very well then I contradict myself. (I am large. I contain multitudes.)"

Janus Words

In the year 1666 a great fire swept through London and destroyed more than half the city, including three-quarters of St. Paul's Cathedral. Sir Christopher Wren, the original designer of the cathedral and perhaps the finest architect of all time, was commissioned to rebuild the great edifice. He began in 1675 and finished in 1710—a remarkably short period of time for such a task. When the magnificent edifice was completed, Queen Anne, the reigning monarch, visited the cathedral and told Wren that his work was "awful, artificial, and amusing." Sir Christopher, so the story goes, was delighted with the royal compliment, because in those days *awful* meant "full of awe, awe-inspiring," *artificial* meant "artistic," and *amusing,* from the *muses,* meant "amazing."

That was three hundred years ago. Today, the older, flattering meanings of *awful, artificial,* and *amusing* have virtually disappeared from popular use. Indeed, the general rule of language is that when a single word develops two polar meanings, one will become obsolete. Occasionally, though, two diametrically opposed meanings of the same English word survive, and the technical term for these same words–opposite meanings pairs is *contronyms.* More popularly, they are known as Janus words because the Roman god Janus had two faces that looked in opposite directions.

Here's a little finger exercise. Remember that I'm the teacher, so you must try to do what I ask. Make a circle with the fingers on your left hand by touching the tip of your index finger to the tip of your thumb. Now poke your head through that circle.

If you unsuccessfully tried to fit your head through the small digital circle, you (and almost any reader) thought that the phrase "poke your head" meant that your head was the poker. But if you raised your left hand with the circle of fingers up close to your forehead and poked your right index finger through that circle until it touched your forehead, you realized that the phrase "poke your head" has a second, and opposite, meaning: that the head is the pokee.

Here are two sentences that will solidify your understanding of how Janus words work:

The moon is VISIBLE *tonight.*

The lights in the old house are always INVISIBLE.

Although the two capitalized words are opposite in meaning, both can be replaced by the same word—*out*. When the moon or sun or stars are out, they are visible. When the lights are out, they are invisible.

Here are some contronymic sentences that show how words wander wondrously and testify to the fact that nothing in the English language is absolute:

bolt. to secure in place; to dart away: *a*. I'll bolt the door. *b*. Did you see the horse bolt?

buckle. fasten together; fall apart: *a*. Safe drivers buckle their seat belts. *b*. Unsafe buildings buckle at the slightest tremor of the earth.

burn. to destroy; to create: *a*. Let's burn the evidence. *b*. Let's burn a CD.

certain. definite; difficult to specify: *a*. I am certain about what I want in life. *b*. I have a certain feeling about the plan.

cleave. separate; adhere firmly: *a*. A strong blow will cleave a plank in two. *b*. Bits of metal cleave to a magnet.

clip. fasten; separate: *a*. Clip the coupon to the newspaper. *b*. Clip the coupon from the newspaper.

commencement. beginning; conclusion: *a*. Beautiful weather marked the commencement of spring. *b*. She won an award at her high school commencement.

critical. opposed; essential to: *a.* Joanne is critical of our effort. *b.* Joanne is critical to our effort.

dress. put items on; remove items from: *a.* Let's dress for the ball. *b.* Let's dress the chicken for cooking.

dust. remove material from; spread material on: *a.* Three times a week they dust the floor. *b.* Three times each season they dust the crops.

fast. firmly in one place; rapidly from one place to another: *a.* The pegs held the tent fast. *b.* She ran fast.

fix. restore; remove part of: *a.* It's time to fix the fence. *b.* It's time to fix the bull.

give out. produce; stop producing: *a.* A good furnace will give out enough energy to heat the house. *b.* A broken furnace will often give out.

handicap. advantage; disadvantage: *a.* What's your handicap in golf? *b.* His lack of education is a handicap.

hold up. support; hinder: *a.* Please hold up the sagging branch. *b.* Accidents hold up the flow of traffic.

impregnable. invulnerable to penetration; able to be impregnated: *a.* The castle was so strongly built that it was impregnable. *b.* Treatments exist for making a childless woman more impregnable.

keep up. continue to fall; continue to stay up: *a.* The farmers hope that the rain will keep up. *b.* Damocles hoped that the sword above his head would keep up.

left. departed from; remaining: *a.* Ten people left the room. *b.* Five people were left in the room.

moot. debatable; not worthy of debate: *a*. Capital punishment is a moot point. *b*. That the Earth revolves around the Sun is a moot point.

mortal. deadly; subject to death: *a*. The knight delivered a mortal blow. *b*. All humans are mortal.

oversight. careful supervision; neglect: *a*. The foreman was responsible for the oversight of the project. *b*. The foreman's oversight ruined the success of the project.

put out. generate; extinguish: *a*. The candle put out enough light for us to see. *b*. Before I went to bed, I put out the candle.

qualified. competent; limited: *a*. The candidate for the job was fully qualified. *b*. The dance was a qualified success.

sanction. give approval of; censure: *a*. The NCAA plans to sanction the event. *b*. Should our country impose a new sanction on Libya?

scan. examine carefully; glance at hastily: *a*. I scan the poem. *b*. Each day, I scan the want ads.

screen. view; hide from view: *a*. Tonight the critics will screen the film. *b*. Defensemen mustn't screen the puck.

seeded. with seeds; without seeds: *a*. The rain nourished the seeded field. *b*. Would you like some seeded raisins?

take. obtain; offer: *a*. Professional photographers take good pictures. *b*. Professional models take good pictures.

temper. soften; strengthen: *a*. You must temper your anger with reason. *b*. Factories temper steel with additives.

think better. admire more; be suspicious of: *a*. I think better of the first proposal than the second. *b*. If I were you, I'd think better of that proposal.

trim. add things to; cut away: *a*. Let's trim the Christmas tree. *b*. Let's trim the hedge.

trip. to stumble; to move gracefully: *a*. Don't trip on the curb. *b*. Let's trip the light fantastic.

unbending. rigid; relaxing: *a*. On the job Smith is completely unbending. *b*. Relaxing on the beach is a good way of unbending.

wear. endure through use; decay through use: *a*. This suit will wear like iron. *b*. Water can cause mountains to wear.

weather. withstand; wear away: *a*. Strong ships weather storms. *b*. Wind can weather rocks.

wind up. start; end: *a*. I have to wind up my watch. *b*. Now I have to wind up this discussion of curious and contrary contronyms.

with. alongside; against: *a*. England fought with France against Germany. *b*. England fought with France.

One of the sharpest tools in the humor kit is the writer's ability to identify an anomaly and to extrapolate it into absurdity. Snatching a handful of irregular plurals in our English language, I was able to shape one of my most extended and, I feel, most sprightly dialogues. Beyond the humor, though, I feel an abiding sadness that our quirkiest and most colorful plural forms—along with so many of our irregular past tense verb forms—are winking out of our language.

Foxen in the Henhice

Recently I undertook an extensive study of American dialects, and a friend told me about a farmer named Eben Pluribus who spoke a most unusual kind of English. So I went to visit Farmer Pluribus, and here is a transcript of our interview:

"Mr. Pluribus, I hear that you've had some trouble on the farm."

"Well, young fella, times were hard for a spell. Almost every night them danged foxen were raiding my henhice."

"Excuse me, sir," I interjected. "Don't you mean foxes?"

"Nope, I don't," Pluribus replied. "I use oxen to plow my fields, so it's foxen that I'm trying to get rid of."

"I see. But what are henhice?" I asked.

"Easy. One mouse, two mice; one henhouse, two henhice. You must be one of them city slickers, but surely you know that henhice are what them birds live in that, when they're little critters, they utter all them peep."

"I think I'm beginning to understand you, Mr. Pluribus. But don't you mean peeps?"

"Nope, I mean peep. More than one sheep is a flock of sheep, and more than one peep is a bunch of peep. What do you think I am, one of them old ceet?"

"I haven't meant to insult you, sir," I gulped. "But I can't quite make out what you're saying."

"Then you must be a touch slow in the head," Farmer Pluribus shot back. "One foot, two feet; one coot, two ceet. I'm just trying to easify the English language, so I make all regular plural nouns irregular. Once they're all irregular, then it's just the same like they're all regular."

"Makes perfect sense to me," I mumbled.

"Good boy," said Pluribus, and a gleam came into his eyes. "Now, as I was trying to explain, them pesky foxen made such a fuss that all the meese and lynges have gone north."

"Aha!" I shouted. "You're talking about those big antlered animals, aren't you? One goose, two geese; one moose, a herd of meese. And lynges is truly elegant—one sphinx, a row of sphinges; one lynx, a litter of lynges."

"You're a smart fella, sonny," smiled Pluribus. "You see, I used to think that my cose might scare away them foxen, but the cose were too danged busy chasing rose."

"Oh, oh. You've lost me again," I lamented. "What are cose and rose?"

"Guess you ain't so smart after all," Pluribus sneered. "If *those* is the plural of *that*, then *cose* and *rose* got to be the plurals of *cat* and *rat*."

"Sorry that I'm so thick, but I'm really not one of those people who talk through their hose," I apologized, picking up Pluribus's cue. "Could you please tell me what happened to the foxen in your henhice?"

"I'd be pleased to," answered Pluribus. "What happened was that my brave wife, Una, grabbed one of them frying pen and took off after them foxen."

I wondered for a moment what frying pen were and soon realized that because the plural of *man* is *men*, the plural of *pan* had to be *pen*.

"Well," Pluribus went right on talking, "the missus wasn't able to catch them foxen so she went back to the kitchen and began throwing dish and some freshly made pice at them critters."

That part of the story stumped me for a time, until I reasoned that a school of fish is made up of fish and more than one die make a roll of dice so that Una Pluribus must have grabbed a stack of dishes and pies.

Pluribus never stopped. "Them dish and pice sure scarified them foxen, and the pests have never come back. In fact, the rest of the village heard about what my wife did, and they were so proud that they sent the town band out to the farm to serenade her with tubae, harmonicae, accordia, fives, and dra."

"Hold up!" I gasped. "Give me a minute to figure out those musical instruments. The plural of *formula* is *formulae*, so the plurals of *tuba* and *harmonica* must be *tubae* and *harmonicae*. And the plurals of *phenomenon* and *criterion* are *phenomena* and *criteria*, so the plural of *accordion* must be *accordia*."

"You must be one of them genii!" Pluribus exclaimed.

"Maybe," I blushed. "One cactus, two cacti; one alumnus, an association of alumni. So one genius, a seminar of genii. But let me get back to those instruments. The plurals of *life* and *wife* are *lives* and *wives*, so the plural of *fife* must be *fives*. And the plural of *medium* is *media*, so the plural of *drum* must be *dra*. Whew! That last one was tough."

"Good boy, sonny. Well, my wife done such a good job of chasing away them foxen that the town newspaper printed up a story and ran a couple of photographim of her holding them pen, dish, and pice."

My brain was now spinning in high gear, so it took me but an instant to realize that Farmer Pluribus had regularized one of the most exotic plurals in the English language—*seraph, seraphim*; so *photograph, photographim*. I could imagine all those Pluribi bathing in their bathtubim, as in *cherub, cherubim; bathtub, bathtubim*.

"Well," crowed Pluribus. "I was mighty pleased that everybody was so nice to the missus, but that ain't no surprise since folks in these here parts show a lot of respect for their methren."

"Brother, brethren; mother, methren," I rejoined. "That thought makes me want to cry. Have you any boxen of Kleenices here?"

"Sure do, young fella. And I'm tickled pink that you've caught on to the way I've easified the English language. One index, two indices, and one appendix, two appendices. So one Kleenex, two Kleenices. Makes things simpler, don't it?"

I was so grateful to Farmer Pluribus for having taught me his unique dialect that I took him out to one of them local cafeteriae. Then I reported my findings to the American Dialect Society by calling from one of the telephone beeth in the place.

Yep, you've got it. One tooth, two teeth. One telephone booth, two telephone beeth. Makes things simpler, don't it?

The ancients knew that the best way to make the med-
icine go down was to coat the rim of the cup with honey.
When I sense that the rhythm and conciseness of verse will
embellish a discussion, I love to create poems that embody
the language concepts that I am trying to explain. The po-
ems in this chapter and at the end of the book are scattered
throughout my work; I'm pleased to have the chance to
gather them together into two exhibits.

A Uni-Verse
of Language

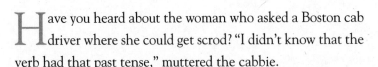

Have you heard about the woman who asked a Boston cab driver where she could get scrod? "I didn't know that the verb had that past tense," muttered the cabbie.

That classic relies on the fact that verb tenses in English appear to be erratic, fraught with a fearful asymmetry and puzzling unpredictability. Some verbs form their past tense by adding *-d*, *-ed*, or *-t*—*walk, walked; bend, bent.* Others go back in time through an internal vowel change—*begin, began; sing,* *sang.* Another cluster adds *-d* or *-t* and undergoes an internal vowel change—*lose, lost; buy, bought.* And still others don't change at all—*set, set; put, put.* No wonder, then, that our eyes glaze and our breath quickens when we have to form the past tense of verbs like *dive, weave, shine, sneak,* and *baby-sit.*

The past tenses of verbs in our language cause so many of us to become tense that I've written a poem about the insanity:

A Tense Time with Verbs

The verbs in English are a fright.
How can we learn to read and write?
Today we speak, but first we spoke;
Some faucets leak, but never loke.
Today we write, but first we wrote;
We bite our tongues, but never bote.

★

Each day I teach, for years I taught,
And preachers preach, but never praught.
This tale I tell; this tale I told;
I smell the flowers, but never smold.

★

If knights still slay, as once they slew,
Then do we play, as once we plew?
If I still do as once I did,
Then do cows moo, as they once mid?

★

I love to win, and games I've won;
I seldom sin, and never son.
I hate to lose, and games I lost;
I didn't choose, and never chost.

★

I love to sing, and songs I sang;
I fling a ball, but never flang.
I strike that ball, that ball I struck;
This poem I like, but never luck.

★

I take a break, a break I took;
I bake a cake, but never book.
I eat that cake, that cake I ate;
I beat an egg, but never bate.

★

I often swim, as I once swam;
I skim some milk, but never skam.
I fly a kite that I once flew;
I tie a knot, but never tew.

★

I see the truth, the truth I saw;
I flee from falsehood, never flaw.
I stand for truth, as I once stood;
I land a fish, but never lood.

★

About these verbs I sit and think.
These verbs don't fit. They seem to wink
At me, who sat for years and thought
Of verbs that never fat or wought.

The most universally confused pair of verbs in English is *lay* and *lie*. When the Enron Corporation scandal broke in early 2002 and I noted the last name of the disgraced CEO, Kenneth Lay, a little quatrain immediately knocked on the door of my imagination and said, "Write me!":

Take the Money Enron
*The difference between **lie** and **lay***
Has fallen into deep decay.
But now we know from Enron's shame
*That **Lay** and **lie** are just the same.*

Linguists Otto Jespersen and Mario Pei have branded English spelling as a "pseudohistorical and antieducational abomination" that is "the world's most awesome mess." The chasm that stretches between how words are spelled and how they actually sound is best illustrated by the letter combination *–ough:*

Tough Stough
The wind was rough.
The cold was grough.
She kept her hands
Inside her mough.

★

And even though
She loved the snough,
The weather was
A heartless fough.

★

It chilled her through.
Her lips turned blough.
The frigid flakes
They blough and flough.

★

They shook each bough,
And she saw hough
The animals froze—
Each cough and sough.

★

While at their trough,
Just drinking brough,
Were frozen fast
Each slough and mough.

★

It made her hiccough—
Worse than a sticcough.
She drank hot cocoa
For an instant piccough.

One of the first spelling formulas we are taught in school is "*i* before *e*, except after *c*." To show how much this rule was made to be broken, I offer a poem that I hope will leave you spellbound:

E-I, I-E—Oh?

There's a rule that's sufficeint, proficeint, efficeint.
For all speceis of spelling in no way deficeint.
While the glaceirs of ignorance icily frown,
This soveriegn rule warms, like a thick iederdown.

★

On words fiesty and wierd it shines from great hieghts,
Blazes out like a beacon, or skien of ieght lights.
It gives nieghborly guidance, sceintific and fair,
To this nonpariel language to which we are hier.

★

Now, a few in soceity fiegn to deride
And to forfiet their anceint and omnisceint guide,
Diegn to worship a diety foriegn and hienous,
Whose counterfiet riegn is certain to pain us.

★

In our work and our liesure, our agenceis, schools,
Let us all wiegh our consceince, sieze proudly our rules!
It's plebiean to lower our standards. I'll niether
Give in or give up—and I trust you won't iether!

Some words just can't buy a vowel—not an *a* or an *e* or an *i* or an *o* or a *u*. With tongue firmly planted in cheek, some call these words that have had a vowel removement "abstemious" words—a facetious label since *abstemious* (along with *facetious*) contains every major vowel, and in sequence.

In the poem you're about to read, you'll find a heavenly three-syllable word that eschews the major vowels—*syzygy,* which means "the nearly straight-line configuration of three celestial bodies."

A Sonnet to Abstemious Words

Once did a shy but spry gypsy
Spy a pygmy, who made him feel tipsy.
Her form, like a lynx, sylph, and nymph,
Made all his dry glands feel quite lymph.

★

He felt so in synch with her rhythm
That he hoped she'd fly to the sky with him.
No sly myth would he try on her,
Preferring to ply her with myrrh.

★

When apart, he would fry and then cry,
Grow a cyst and a sty in his eye.
That's why they would tryst at the gym,
By a crypt, where he'd write a wry hymn.

★

Her he loved to the nth degree,
Like a heavenly syzygy.

A capitonym is a word that changes meaning and pronunciation when it is capitalized, as illustrated in the next two quatrains:

Job's Job

*In **August,** an **august** patriarch,*
*Was **reading** an ad in **Reading,** Mass.*
*Long-suffering **Job** secured a **job***
*To **polish** piles of **Polish** brass.*

★

Herb's Herbs

*An **herb** store owner, name of **Herb,***
*Moved to **rainier** Mt. **Rainier.***
*It would have been so **nice** in **Nice,***
*And even **tangier** in **Tangier.***

As you read the next poem, note the unusual pattern of the end-rhymes:

Listen, readers, toward me bow.
Be friendly; do not draw the bow.
Please don't try to start a row.
Sit peacefully, all in a row.
Don't squeal like a big, fat sow.
Do not the seeds of discord sow.

Even though each couplet ends with the same word, the rhymes occur on every other line. That's because *bow, row,* and *sow* each possess two different pronunciations and spellings. These rare pairings are called heteronyms:

A Hymn to Heteronyms

*Please come through the **entrance** of this little poem.*
*I guarantee it will **entrance** you.*
*The **content** will certainly make you **content**,*
And the knowledge gained sure will enhance you.

★

*A boy **moped** around when his parents refused*
*For him a new **moped** to buy.*
*The **incense** he burned did **incense** him to go*
*On a **tear** with a **tear** in his eye.*

★

*He **ragged** on his parents, felt they ran him **ragged**.*
*His just **deserts** they never gave.*
*He imagined them out on some **deserts** so dry,*
Where for water they'd search and they'd rave.

★

*At **present** he just won't **present** or **converse***
*On the **converse** of each high-flown theory*
*Of circles and **axes** in math class; he has*
*Many **axes** to grind, isn't cheery.*

★

*He tried to play baseball, but often **skied** out,*
*So when the snows came, he just **skied**.*
*He then broke a leg **putting** on his ski boots,*
*And his **putting** in golf was in need.*

★

*He once held the **lead** in a cross-country race,*
*Till, his legs started feeling like **lead**,*

And when the pain **peaked,** he looked kind of **peaked.**
His **liver** felt **liver,** then dead.

★

A **number** of times he felt **number,** all **wound**
Up, like one with a **wound,** not a wand.
His new TV **console** just couldn't **console**
Or **slough** off a **slough** of despond.

★

The **rugged** boy paced 'round his shaggy-**rugged** room,
And he spent the whole **evening** till dawn
Evening out the cross**winds** of his hate.
Now my anecdote **winds** on and on.

★

He thought: "**Does** the prancing of so many **does**
Explain why down **dove** the white **dove,**
Or why **pussy** cat has a **pussy** old sore
And **bass** sing in **bass** notes of their love?"

★

Do they always sing, "**Do** re mi" and stare, **agape,**
At eros, **agape,** each **minute?**
Their love's not **minute;** there's an **overage** of love.
Even **overage** fish are quite in it.

★

These bass fish have never been in short **supply**
As they **supply** spawn without waiting.
With their love fluids bubbling, abundant, **secretive,**
There's many a **secretive** mating.

The Write Way

Literature is a special kind of language that catches and crystallizes our lives. Thus, lovers of language are usually lovers of literature. I am. I've never found another entertainment that is as cheap and accessible as reading, nor any pleasure so lasting.

The first bookmobile in history was, perhaps, the property of the Dutch humanist writer Desiderius Erasmus, who created the first bestseller, In Praise of Folly. Erasmus had few personal possessions outside of his books, and he declared: "When I get a little money, I buy books; and if any is left, I buy food and clothes. My luggage is my library. My home is where my books are." No surprise, then, that in Erasmus's caravan during his travels throughout sixteenth-century Europe, one donkey was reserved exclusively to carry his books.

When Sir Walter Scott returned to Abbotsford to die, he was wheeled into his library. He burst into tears as he beheld his many lifelong friends arrayed upon his bookshelves. When we take down a book from the shelf, we hear the voice of a friend across time and space, speaking to us mind to mind, heart to heart.

Literature Lives!

Not long ago, a woman telephoned an Atlanta library and asked, "Can you please tell me where Scarlet O'Hara is buried?"

The librarian explained, "Scarlet is a fictional character in Margaret Mitchell's novel *Gone with the Wind*."

"Never mind that," said the caller. "I want to know where she's buried."

For that reader, Scarlet O'Hara had been so alive that she was dead.

Literature lives. Literature endures. Literature prevails. I know this because I know that readers bestow a special kind of life upon people who have existed only in books. Figments though they may be, literary characters can assume a vitality and longevity that pulse more powerfully than flesh and blood. "The strongest memory is weaker than the palest ink," says a Chinese proverb. Anatole Broyard tells us, "A good book is never exhausted. It goes on whispering to you from the wall"; Edward Bulwer-Lytton, "Laws die; books never"; and Franklin Roosevelt, "People die, but books never die. No man and no force can abolish memory."

After many years, the publishers of the children's classic *Charlotte's Web* persuaded E. B. White to record his book on tape. So caught had the author become in the web of his arachnid heroine's life that it took nineteen tapings before White could read aloud the passage about Charlotte's death without his voice cracking.

A century earlier, another writer had been deeply affected by the fate of his heroine. Like most of Charles Dickens's works, *The Old Curiosity Shop* (1841) was published in serial form. The novel won a vast readership on both sides of the Atlantic, and as interest in the fate of the heroine, Little Nell, grew intense, circulation reached the staggering figure of 100,000, a record unequaled by any other of Dickens's major novels. In New York, 6,000 people crowded the wharf where the ship carrying the final *Master Humphrey's Clock* magazine installment was due to dock. As the vessel approached, the crowd's impatience grew to such a pitch that it cried out as one to the sailors, "Does Little Nell die?"

Alas, Little Nell did die, and tens of thousands of readers' hearts broke. The often-ferocious literary critic Lord Jeffrey was found weeping with his head on his library table. "You'll be sorry to hear," he sobbed to a friend, "that little Nelly, Boz's little Nelly, is dead." Daniel O'Connell, an Irish M.P., burst out crying, "He should not have killed her," and then, in anguish, he threw the book out of the window of the train in which he was traveling. A diary of the time records another reader lamenting, "The villain! The rascal! The bloodthirsty scoundrel! He killed my little Nell! He killed my sweet little child!"

That "bloodthirsty scoundrel" was himself shattered by the loss of his heroine. In a letter to a friend, Dickens wrote, "I am the wretchedest of the wretched. It [Nell's death] casts the most horrible shadow upon me, and it is as much as I can do to keep moving at all. Nobody will miss her like I shall."

Even more famous than Charlotte and Little Nell is Arthur Conan Doyle's Sherlock Holmes, the world's first consulting detective. The intrepid sleuth's deerstalker hat, Inverness cape, calabash pipe, and magnifying glass are recognized by readers everywhere, and the stories have been translated into more than sixty languages, from Arabic to Yiddish.

Like the heroes of so many popular stories and myths, Sherlock Holmes was born in poverty and nearly died at birth from neglect. Dr. Arthur Conan Doyle was a novice medical practitioner with a dearth of patients. To while away his time and to help pay a few bills, Doyle took pen in hand and created one of the first detectives to base his work squarely on scientific methods.

The publishing word of 1886 did not grasp the revolutionary implications of Doyle's ideas. Editor after editor returned the manuscript with coldly polite rejection notices. After a year and a half, the young author was about to give up hope, when one publisher finally took a chance and bought the rights for five pounds sterling. In December of 1887, Sherlock Holmes came into the world as an unheralded and unnoticed Yuletide child in *Beeton's Christmas Annual*. When, not long after, *The Strand Magazine* began the monthly serialization of the first dozen short stories, entitled *The Adventures of Sherlock Holmes*, the issues sold tens of thousands of copies, and the public furiously clamored for more.

At the height of his success, however, the creator wearied of his creation. He yearned for "higher writing" and felt his special calling to be the historical novel. In December 1893, Doyle introduced into the last story in the Memoirs series the archcriminal Professor James Moriarty. In "The Final Problem," Holmes and the evil professor wrestle at a cliff's edge in Switzerland. Grasping each other frantically, sleuth and villain plummet to their watery deaths at the foot of the Reichenbach Falls.

With Holmes forever destroyed, Doyle felt he could abandon his mystery stories and turn his authorial eyes to the romantic landscapes of the Middle Ages. He longed to chronicle the clangor of medieval battles, the derring-do of brave knights, and the sighs of lovesick maidens. But the writer's tour back in time would not be that easily booked: Sherlock Holmes had taken on a life of his own, something larger than the will of his creator. The normally staid, stiff-upper-lipped British public first felt bereaved, then outraged. Conservative London stockbrokers went to work wearing black armbands in mourning for the loss of their heroic detective. Citizens poured out torrents of letters to editors complaining of Holmes's fate. One woman picketed Doyle's home with a sign branding him a murderer.

The appeals of *The Strand*'s publishers to Doyle's sensibilities and purse went unheeded. For the next eight years Holmes lay dead at the bottom of the Swiss falls while Doyle branched out into historical fiction, science fiction, horror stories, and medical stories. But he wasn't very good at "higher writing."

Finally, Doyle could resist the pressures from publisher and public no more. He wrote what may be the best of all the Holmes stories, "The Hound of the Baskervilles," which was immediately serialized in *The Strand*. As the story made clear, Holmes had not returned from his demise as reported in 1893. This tale was merely a reminiscence, set in 1888. Still, the reappearance of Sherlock Holmes fired the public imagination and enthusiasm; readers again queued up by the thousands to buy the monthly installments of the magazine. In 1903, ten years after his "death," Doyle's detective rose up from his watery grave in the Reichenbach Falls, his logical wonders to perform for the whole world.

The Return of Sherlock Holmes, the series of thirteen stories that brought back Doyle's hero, was greeted eagerly by patient British readers whose appetites had been whetted by "Hound," and the author continued writing stories of his detective right into 1927. When, in 1930, Arthur Conan Doyle died at age seventy-one, readers around the world mourned his passing. Newspaper cartoons portraying a grieving Sherlock Holmes captured the public's sense of irreparable loss.

Such is the power of mythic literature that the creation has outlived his creator. Letters and packages from all over the world still come addressed to "Sherlock Holmes" at 221-B Baker Street, where they are answered by a full-time secretary. Only Santa Claus gets more mail, at least just before Christmastime. More movies—well over three hundred of them—have been made about Holmes than about Dracula, Frankenstein, Robin Hood, and Rocky combined. Sherlock Holmes stories written by post-Doylean authors now vastly outnumber the sixty that Doyle produced. More than 150 societies in homage to Sherlock Holmes are active in the United States alone.

However many times the progenitor tried to finish off his hero, by murder or retirement or flat refusal to write any more adventures, the Great Detective lives, vigilant and deductive as ever, protecting the humble from the evils that lurk in the very heart of our so-called civilization. Despite his "death" a hundred years ago, Sherlock Holmes has never died. Readers around the world simply won't let him.

Benjamin Franklin was a guest at a Paris dinner party when a question was posed: What condition of man most deserves pity? Each guest proposed an example of a miserable situation. When Franklin's turn came, he responded, "A lonesome man on a rainy day who does not know how to read." Because you are still holding this volume in your hand, you must be a bibliophile. As a member of that happy and privileged band, you will never be lonely. Forevermore you have the company and conversation of thousands of men and women, ancient and contemporary, learned and light, who have set their humanity to paper and crafted language into literature.

I hope you'll find this game a novel way of reviewing the classics. This challenge will also remind you of how violent great literature can be.

Still Hot off the Press

E zra Pound once defined literature as "news that stays news." The plots spun out by many classic works of litera-ture are as contemporary as today's headlines, especially as they are screamed in the tabloids. Just think what the *National Enquirer* and *Star* would do with the stories told in famous books if they had actually happened. What literary plots are reflected in the following lurid headlines? Name the author who wrote each grisly tale:

1. KING KILLS HIS FATHER, THEN MARRIES WOMAN
   OLD ENOUGH TO BE HIS MOTHER—AND SHE IS!

   ★

2. VERONA TEENAGERS COMMIT DOUBLE SUICIDE;
   FAMILIES VOW TO END CLAN VENDETTA

   ★

3. GARAGE OWNER STALKS
AFFLUENT BUSINESSMAN,
THEN SHOTGUNS HIM
IN HIS SWIMMING POOL

★

4. DOCTOR'S WIFE AND LOCAL MINISTER EXPOSED
FOR CONCEIVING ILLEGITIMATE DAUGHTER

★

5. COLLAR FACTORY EMLOYEE CONVICTED
OF DROWNING PREGNANT GIRLFRIEND

★

6. CHICAGO CHAUFFEUR SMOTHERS
BOSS'S DAUGHTER, THEN CUTS HER UP
AND STUFFS HER IN FURNACE

★

7. STUDENT CONFESSES TO AXE MURDER
OF LOCAL PAWNBROKER AND ASSISTANT

★

8. MADWOMAN LONG IMPRISONED IN ATTIC
SETS HOUSE ON FIRE, THEN LEAPS TO DEATH

★

9. FORMER SCHOOLTEACHER FOUND
TO HAVE BEEN LOOSE WOMAN,
COMMITTED TO INSANE ASYLUM

★

10. GOVT. OFFICIAL'S WIFE,
BEARING COUNT'S CHILD,
FLINGS SELF UNDER TRAIN

★

11. GHOSTS OF FORMER SERVANTS
HAUNT GOVERNESS, CHILDREN

★

12. SKELETON OF WINE TASTER DISCOVERED
BEHIND BRICK WALL IN MANSION CELLAR

★

13. RETARDED ITINERANT FARMWORKER
CRUSHES BOSS'S DAUGHTER-IN-LAW;
THEN MERCY-KILLED BY BEST FRIEND

★

14. MAYOR FOUND TO HAVE AUCTIONED
OFF WIFE AND DAUGHTER TO SAILOR

★

15. STEPMOTHER STRANGLES HER BABY
TO PROVE LOVE FOR HER STEPSON;
BOTH GIVE THEMSELVES UP

★

16. SMITTEN BY MULTIPLE-PERSONALITY DISORDER,
PROMINENT LONDON DOCTOR KILLS SELVES

★

17. MAROONED ON CORAL ISLAND,
BRITISH PREPPIES KILL EACH OTHER

★

18. WOMAN RAISED IN CONVENT,
CAUGHT IN WEB OF SEX
AND DEBT, TAKES ARSENIC

★

19. PRINCE ACQUITTED OF KILLING MOTHER
IN REVENGE FOR MURDER OF HIS FATHER

★

20. BRIDGE IN PERU COLLAPSES;
FIVE PLUNGE TO THEIR DEATHS

★

21. DENTIST WHO BLUDGEONED WIFE FOUND DEAD
IN DEATH VALLEY HANDCUFFED TO PURSUER

★

22. MOTHER PLOTS MERCY KILLING OF SON
AFFLICTED WITH A SOCIAL DISEASE

★

23. WOMAN KNITS WHOLE WARDROBES
DURING PUBLIC EXECUTIONS

★

24. LORD OF MANOR FRIGHTENED TO DEATH
BY PHOSPHORESCENT GIANT DOG

★

25. MASS. ADULTERERS SURVIVE DUAL SUICIDE PACT;
ATTEMPTED TO RAM THEIR SLED INTO TREE

Answers

1. Sophocles, *Oedipus Rex* 2. William Shakespeare, *Romeo and Juliet* 3. F. Scott Fitzgerald, *The Great Gatsby* 4. Nathaniel Hawthorne, *The Scarlet Letter* 5. Theodore Dreiser, *An American Tragedy* 6. Richard Wright, *Native Son* 7. Fyodor Dostoevsky, *Crime and Punishment* 8. Charlotte Brontë, *Jane Eyre* 9. Tennessee Williams, *A Streetcar Named Desire* 10. Leo Tolstoy, *Anna Karenina*

11. Henry James, *The Turn of the Screw* 12. Edgar Allan Poe, "The Cask of Amontillado" 13. John Steinbeck, *Of Mice and Men* 14. Thomas Hardy, *The Mayor of Casterbridge* 15. Eugene O'Neill, *Desire Under the Elms* 16. Robert Louis Stevenson, *The Strange Case of Dr. Jekyll and Mr. Hyde* 17. William Golding, *Lord of the Flies* 18. Gustave Flaubert, *Madame Bovary* 19. Aeschylus, *Eumenides* (in *Oresteiâ*) 20. Thornton Wilder, *The Bridge of San Luis Rey* 21. Frank Norris, *McTeague* 22. Henrik Ibsen, *Ghosts* 23. Charles Dickens, *A Tale of Two Cities* 24. Arthur Conan Doyle, "The Hound of the Baskervilles" 25. Edith Wharton, *Ethan Frome*

In Romeo and Juliet *and other plays and poems,*
William Shakespeare invented the theme of romantic love
between real people. Others had spun stories of love be-
tween men and women found on altarpieces and stained-
glass windows, but no English-language writer before
Shakespeare had plumbed the depths of love and passion
between flesh-and-blood and bone-and-hair human beings.
Along the way, Shakespeare also invented our language.
No surprise to you, I hope, that from among my writings
about great authors, I have chosen for this collection this
tribute to this author.

A Man of
Fire-New Words

What do these four sentences have in common?:

Has Will a peer, I ask me.
I swear he's like a lamp.
We all make his praise.
Ah, I speak a swell rime.

Each is an anagram that uses all the letters in the name *William Shakespeare* and captures a luminous truth: Peerless Will Shakespeare shines through the centuries and inspires our praise.

Little information about William Shakespeare's personal life is available, but from municipal records we can deduce that he was born in the English village of Stratford-upon-Avon, in the county of Warwickshire, on April 23, 1564, and that having retired to his hometown around 1611, he died there on April 23, 1616. Shakespeare's plays, which he wrote in London between approximately 1590 and 1613, have been in almost-constant production since their creation. Because the playwright dealt with universal truths and conflicts in human nature, his tragedies, comedies, and history plays continue to draw audiences from all walks of life, just as they did in their own day. Time has proven the truth of what Shakespeare's contemporary, Ben Jonson, said of him: "He was not of an age, but for all time."

An often-neglected aspect of William Shakespeare's genius is that his words, as well as his works, were not just of an age, but for all time. He was, quite simply, the greatest wordmaker who ever lived. Ongoing research demonstrates that there are 20,138 lemmata (dictionary headwords) in Shakespeare's published works. That figure represents approximately 40 percent of the total recorded for the English language up to the year 1623—and Shakespeare could not have owned any dictionary in which he could have looked up these words! For purposes of comparison, bear in mind that the written vocabulary of Homer totals approximately 9,000 words, that of the King James Bible 8,000, and that of Milton 10,000.

Of the 20,138 basewords that Shakespeare employs in his plays, sonnets, and other poems, his is the first known use of over 1,700 of them. The most verbally innovative of our authors and our all-time champion neologizer, Shakespeare made up more than 8.5 percent of his written vocabulary. Reading his works is like witnessing the birth of language itself.

"I pitied thee, / Took pains to make thee speak," says Prospero to Caliban in *The Tempest*. "I endow'd thy purposes / With words that made them known." Shakespeare is our Prospero; he dressed our thoughts with words and teemed our tongue with phrases. Without him, our "native English" would be, as Thomas Mowbray says in *Richard II*:

> *an unstringed viol or a harp,*
> *Or like a cunning instrument cas'd up—*
> *Or being open, put into his hands*
> *That knows no touch to tune the harmony.*

Consider the following list of fifty representative words that, as far as we can tell, Shakespeare was the first to use in writing. So great is his influence on his native tongue that we find it hard to imagine a time when these words did not exist:

accommodation	hurry
aerial	impartial
amazement	indistinguishable
apostrophe	invulnerable
assassination	lapse
auspicious	laughable
baseless	lonely
bedroom	majestic
bump	misplaced
castigate	monumental
clangor	multitudinous
countless	obscene
courtship	pedant
critic (and critical)	perusal
dexterously	pious
dishearten	premeditated
dislocate	radiance
dwindle	reliance
eventful	road
exposure	sanctimonious
fitful	seamy
frugal	sneak
generous	sportive
gloomy	submerge
gnarled	useless

Now add to these individual words Shakespeare's daring originality with compounds. He created such splendid audacities as *proud-pied April, heaven-kissing hill,* and *world-without-end hour,* and he bequeathed to the English language such now-familiar double plays as *barefaced, civil tongue, cold comfort, eyesore, faint-hearted, fancy-free, foregone conclusion, father Time, foul play* (and *fair play*), *green-eyed, half-cocked, heartsick, high time, hot-blooded, itching palm, lackluster, laughingstock, leapfrog, lie low, long-haired, love affair, ministering angel, pitched battle, primrose path, sea change, short shrift, snow-white, stony-hearted, tongue-tied, towering passion,* and *yeoman's service.* The striking compound that Shakespeare fashioned to describe Don Adriano de Armando in *Love's Labour's Lost* is an appropriate epithet for the playwright himself: "a man of fire-new words."

Oscar Wilde once quipped, "Now we sit through Shakespeare in order to recognize the quotations." Unrivaled in so many other ways in matters verbal, Shakespeare is unequaled as a phrasemaker. "All for one, one for all," and "not a creature was stirring, not even a mouse," respectively wrote Alexandre Dumas in *The Three Musketeers* and Clement Clark Moore in "The Night Before Christmas." But Shakespeare said them first—"One for all, or all for one we gage" in "The Rape of Lucrece" and "not a mouse stirring" in *Hamlet.*

A student who attended a performance of *Hamlet* came away complaining that the play "was nothing more than a bunch of clichés." The reason for this common reaction is that so many of the memorable expressions in *Hamlet* have become proverbial. In that one play alone were born *brevity is the soul of wit; there's the rub; to thine own self be true; it smells to heaven; the very witching time of night; the primrose path; though this be madness, yet there is method in it; dog will have his day; the apparel oft proclaims the man; neither a borrower nor a lender be; frailty, thy name is woman; something is rotten in the state of Denmark; more honored in the breach than the observance; hoist with his own petard; the lady doth protest too much; to be or not to be; sweets for the sweet; the be-all and end-all; to the manner born; and more in sorrow than in anger.*

Cudgel your brain, and you can append a sample of everyday, idiomatic phrases from other Shakespearean plays: If you knit your brow and wish that this disquisition would vanish into thin air because it is Greek to you, you are quoting William Shakespeare in all his infinite variety. If you point the finger at strange bedfellows and blinking idiots, you are converting Shakespeare's coinages into currency. If you have seen better days in your salad days, when you wore your heart on your sleeve, you are, whether you know it or not, going from Bard to verse. If you break the ice with one fell swoop, if you never stand on ceremonies, if you play it fast and loose until the crack of doom, if you paint the lily, if you hope for a plague on both houses, if you are more sinned against than sinning because you have been eaten out of house and home by your own flesh and blood (the most unkindest cut of all), if you haven't slept a wink and are breathing your last because you're in a pickle, if you carry within you the milk of human kindness and a heart of gold (even though you know that all that glisters is not gold), if you laugh yourself into stitches at too much of a good thing, if you make a virtue of necessity, if you know that the course of true love never did run smooth, and if you won't budge an inch—why, if the truth be told and the truth will out, what the dickens, in a word, right on!, be that as it may, the game is up—you are, as luck would have it, standing on that tower of strength of phrasemakers, William Shakespeare.

Shakespeare lurks in the most astonishing places. Some assert that the Porter's speech in Act 2, scene 3 of *Macbeth* is the source of the modern knock-knock joke: "Knock, knock, knock. Who's there i' th' name of Beelzebob? . . . Knock, knock. Who's there in th' other devil's name? . . . Knock, knock, knock. Who's there? Never at quiet!" And, if you look hard, you can find Shakespeare peeking out even from the pages of the Bible.

The most famous of all biblical translations is the King James Version, the brainchild of James I, who fancied himself a scholar and theologian. The king decided to assure his immortality by sponsoring a new Bible worthy of the splendor of his kingdom. To this end, James appointed a commission of fifty-four learned clerical and lay scholars, divided into three groups in Cambridge, Westminster, and Oxford. Three years of loving labor, 1608–11, produced what John Livingston Lowes called "the noblest monument of English prose." Few readers would dissent from that verdict.

Among the many wonders of the King James Bible is that it stands as one of the few great accomplishments achieved by a committee. At the same time, some commentators have wondered why William Shakespeare was apparently not included among the fifty-four translators chosen. After all,

Shakespeare had already written *Macbeth* in honor of King James (who also fancied himself an expert on witchcraft), and what better committee member to work with the greatest collection of religious literature of all ages than the age's greatest poet?

But an intriguing peculiarity in the King James Bible indicates that Shakespeare was *not* entirely absent from the monumental project. No one knows who made the astonishing discovery or how on earth he or she did it.

In 1610, the year of the most intensive work on the translation, Shakespeare was forty-six years old. Given this clue, we turn to the Forty-sixth Psalm as it appears in the King James Bible. Count down to the forty-sixth word from the beginning and then count up to the forty-sixth word from the end, excluding the cadential *Selah*:

God is our refuge and strength, a very present help in trouble.
Therefore will not we fear, though the earth be removed,
and though the mountains be carried into the midst of the sea;
Though the waters thereof roar and be troubled,
though the mountains shake with the swelling thereof. Selah.
There is a river, the streams whereof shall make glad the city of God,
the holy place of the tabernacle of the Most High.
God is in the midst of her; she shall not be moved:
God shall help her, and that right early.
The heathen raged, the kingdoms were moved:
he uttered his voice, the earth melted.
The Lord of hosts is with us; the God of Jacob is our refuge. Selah.

Come, behold the works of the Lord,
what desolations he hath made on earth;
He maketh wars to cease unto the end of the earth;
he breaketh the bow, and cutteth the spear in sunder;
he burneth the chariot in the fire.
Be still, and know that I am God:
I will be exalted among the heathen, I will be exalted in the earth.
The Lord of hosts is with us; the God of Jacob is our refuge. Selah.

If you counted accurately, your finger eventually lit upon the two words *shake* and *spear*. Shakespeare. Whether or not he created the majesty of the Forty-sixth Psalm, he is in it. Whether the embedded *shake spear* is a purposeful plant or the product of happy chance, the name of the world's most famous poet reposes cunningly in the text of the world's most famous translation.

Shakespeare also hides in many works of twentieth-century literature. He was a busy and prolific writer who, in twenty-five years, turned out thirty-seven long plays and coauthored several others, yet he still found time to provide titles for their books to generations of authors who return again and again to the well of his felicitous phrasing.

Take *Macbeth*, for example. Near the end of the play, Macbeth expresses his darkening vision of life: "It is a tale / Told by an idiot, full of sound and fury, / Signifying nothing." Centuries later, William Faulkner purloined a phrase from that speech for his novel *The Sound and the Fury*, which is indeed told by an idiot, Benjy Compson. Earlier in the play one of the witches chants, "By the pricking of my thumbs, / Something wicked this way comes." Agatha Christie plucked the first line and Ray Bradbury the second as titles of their bestsellers. Other steals from just the one play *Macbeth* include Robert Frost's "Out, Out—," Rose Macaulay's *Told by an Idiot*, Ellis Middleton's *Vaulting Ambition*, Adrienne Rich's *Of Woman Born*, Ngaio Marsh's *Light Thickens*, Anne Sexton's *All My Pretty Ones*, Alistair MacLean's *The Way to Dusty Death*, Edward G. Robinson's *All Our Yesterdays*, Philip Barry's *Tomorrow and Tomorrow*, Malcolm Evans's *Signifying Nothing*, and John Steinbeck's *The Moon Is Down*.

From three other high school favorites—*Julius Caesar, Hamlet*, and *Romeo and Juliet*—have been lifted the titles of Robert Stone's *The Dogs of War*, James Barrie's *Dear Brutus*, John Gunther's *Taken at the Flood*, Barry Sadler's *Cry Havoc*, R. Lance Hill's *The Evil That Men Do*, H. Hall's *The Valiant*, David Halberstam's *Noblest Roman*, A. G. MacDonnell's *How Like an Angel*, Rex Stout's *How like a God*, Joyce Martins' *Rosemary for Remembrance*, Robert B. Parker's *Perchance to Dream*, Arthur Schnitzler's *Undiscovered Country*, Ernest Hebert's *A Little More than Kin*, Edith Wharton's *The Glimpses of the Moon*, Philip K. Dick's *Time out of Joint*, Ogden Nash's *The Primrose Path*, Richard Yates's *A Special Providence*, Frederic Manning's *Her Privates, We*, Tom Stoppard's *Rosencrantz and Guildenstern Are Dead*, Louis Auchincloss's *The Indifferent Children*, Maxwell Anderson's *Both Your Houses*, Eric Knight's *This Above All*, Dorothy Parker's *Not So Deep as a Well*, Ford Madox Ford's *It Was the Nightingale*, Frederick Reynolds's *Fortune's Fool*, and Henry Wade's *No Friendly Drop*.

Add to these Aldous Huxley's *Brave New World* (*The Tempest*); W. Somerset Maugham's *Cakes and Ale* (*Twelfth Night*), John Steinbeck's *The Winter of Our Discontent* (*Richard III*), and dozens of other bardic titles—and it becomes evident that William Shakespeare was one of the most generous souls who ever set quill to parchment. Although he himself was never granted a title, he freely granted titles to others.

The etymologist Ernest Weekley said of Shakespeare, "His contribution to our phraseology is ten times greater than that of any writer to any language in the history of the world." The essayist and novelist Walter Pater exclaimed, "What a garden of words!" In Sonnet CXVI the Bard himself wrote, "If this be error and upon me proved, / I never writ, nor no man ever loved." If Shakespeare had not lived and written with such a loving ear for the music of our language, our English tongue would be immeasurably the poorer. No day goes by that we do not speak and hear and read and write his legacy.

Writers have come up with many a lamentation about how hard it is to be a writer: "I love being a writer. I just can't stand the paperwork," quips Peter De Vries. "Writing is the hardest way of earning a living," observes Olin Miller, "with the possible exception of wrestling alligators." "Writing a book is a horrible, exhausting struggle, like a long bout of some painful illness," moans Winston Churchill. "Writing is easy," explains Gene Fowler. "All you have to do is stare at a blank piece of paper until drops of blood form on your forehead." You get the idea.

I prefer to sing the joys of writing. Almost always I have a terrific time doing it. It feels good, and I like how writing expands my mission of teachership. Here's an extended metaphor—analogy, if you will—that paints my feelings about what Dylan Thomas calls "my craft or sullen art."

Writing Is . . .

For me, writing is like throwing a Frisbee.

You can play Frisbee catch with yourself, but it's repetitious and not much fun. Better it is to fling to others, to extend yourself across a distance.

At first, your tossing is awkward and strengthless. But, with time and practice and maturity, you learn to set your body and brain and heart at the proper angles, to grasp with just the right force and not to choke the missile. You discover how to flick the release so that all things loose and wobbly snap together at just the right moment. You learn to reach out your follow-through hand to the receiver to ensure the straightness and justice of the flight.

And on the just-right days, when the sky is blue and the air pulses with perfect stillness, all points of the Frisbee spin together within their bonded circle—and the object glides on its own whirling, a whirling invisible and inaudible to all others but you.

Like playing Frisbee, writing is a re-creation-al joy. For me, a lot of the fun is knowing that readers out there—you among them—are sharing what I have made. I marvel that, as you pass your eyes over these words, you experience ideas and emotions similar to what I was thinking and feeling when, in another place and another time, I struck the symbols on my keyboard.

Like a whirling, gliding Frisbee, my work extends me beyond the frail confines of my body. Thank you for catching me.

I am one among those writers who take pleasure in writing about writing. If you ask writers how they write and how they are able to keep on writing, you'll get as many answers as the number of writers you ask. Here's how others have done it and how I do it.

How I Write

Ernest Hemingway's first rule for writers was to apply the seat of the pants to the seat of the chair. But not all authors are able to survive with such a simple approach.

Emile Zola pulled the shades and composed by artificial light. Francis Bacon, we are told, knelt each day before creating his greatest works. Martin Luther could not write unless his dog was lying at his feet, while Ben Jonson needed to hear his cat purring. Marcel Proust sealed out the world by lining the walls of his study with cork. Gertrude Stein and Raymond Carver wrote in their cars, while Edmond Rostand preferred to write in his bathtub. Emily Dickinson hardly ever left her home and garden. Wallace Stevens composed poetry while walking to and from work each day at a Hartford insurance company. Alexander Pope and Jean Racine could not write without first declaiming at the top of their voices. Jack Kerouac began each night of writing by kneeling in prayer and composing by candlelight. Friedrich Schiller started each of his writing sessions by opening the drawer of his desk and breathing in the fumes of the rotten apples he had stashed there.

Some writers have donned and doffed gay apparel. Early in his career, John Cheever wore a business suit as he traveled from his apartment to a room in his basement. Then he hung the suit on a hanger and wrote in his underwear. Jessamyn West wrote in bed without getting dressed, as, from time to time, did Eudora Welty, Edith Wharton, Mark Twain, and Truman Capote. John McPhee worked in his bathrobe and tied its sash to the arms of his chair to keep from even thinking about deserting his writing room.

For stimulation, Honoré de Balzac wrote in a monk's costume and drank at least twenty cups of coffee a day, eventually dying of caffeine poisoning. As his vision failed, James Joyce took to wearing a milkman's uniform when he wrote, believing that its whiteness caught the sunlight and reflected it onto his pages. Victor Hugo went to the opposite lengths to ensure his daily output of words on paper. He gave all his clothes to his servant with orders that they be returned only after he had finished his day's quota.

Compared to such strategies, my daily writing regimen is drearily normal. Perhaps that's because I'm a nonfictionalist— a hunter-gatherer of language who records the sounds that escape from the holes in people's faces, leak from their pens, and luminesce up on their computer screens. I don't drink coffee. Rotten fruit doesn't inspire (literally "breathe into") me. My lifelong, heels-over-head love affair with language is my natural caffeine and fructose.

To be a writer, one must behave as writers behave. They write. And write. And write. The difference between a writer and a wannabe is that a writer is someone who can't not write, while a wannabe says, "One of these days when . . . , then I'll. . . ." Unable not to write, I write every day that I'm home.

A grocer doesn't wait to be inspired to go to the store and a banker to go to the bank. I can't afford the luxury of waiting to be inspired before I go to work. Writing is my job, and it happens to be a job that almost nobody gives up on purpose. I love my job as a writer, so I write. Every day that I can.

Long ago, I discovered that I would never become the Great American Novelist. I stink at cobbling characters, dialogue, episode, and setting. You won't find much of that fictional stuff in my books, unless the story serves the ideas I am trying to communicate. A writer has to find out what kind of writer he or she is, and I somehow got born an English teacher with an ability to illuminate ideas about language and literature.

Jean-Jacques Rousseau wrote only in the early morning, Alain-René Lesage only at midday, and Lord Byron only at midnight. Early on, I also discovered that I am more lark than owl—more a morning person than a night person—and certainly not a bat, one who writes through the night. I usually hit the ground punning at around 7:30 A.M., and I'm banging away at the keyboard within an hour.

I write very little on paper, almost everything on my computer. Theodore Sturgeon once wrote, "Nine-tenths of everything is crap." The computer allows me to dump crap into the hard drive without the sense of permanence that handwriting or type on paper used to signify to me. I'm visual and shape my sentences and paragraphs most dexterously on a screen. The computer has not only trebled my output. It has made me a more joyful, liberated, and better writer.

Genetic and environmental roulette has allowed me to work in either a silent or a noisy environment. I'm a speaker as well as a writer, so phone calls and faxes and e-messages chirp and hum and buzz in my writing room, and I often have to answer them during those precious morning hours. That's all right with me. Fictionalists shut the world out. Fictionalists live with their imaginary characters, who get skittish and may flee a noisy room. As I cobble my essays, my readers are my companions, and they will usually stay with me in my writing space through outerworldly alarms and excursions.

Besides, the business of the writing business gives me the privilege of being a writer. In fact, I consider the writing only about half my job. Writers don't make a living writing books. They make a living selling books. After all, I do have to support my writing habit.

When you are heels over head in love with what you do, you never work a day. That's me: butt over teakettle in love with being a writer—a job that nobody who works it would give up on purpose.

Back in 1726, Jonathan Swift took readers of his Gulliver's Travels on voyages to fantastic places peopled by the likes of six-inch-tall men and women and talking horses. In one of those countries, Brobdingnag, the inhabitants are ten times taller than we are, but they keep their language spare and simple: "No law of that country must exceed in words the number of letters in their alphabet; which consists only of two and twenty. They are expressed in the most plain and simple terms, wherein those people are not mercurial enough to discover above one interpretation." Lemuel Gulliver's observation is now almost three centuries old, but so few of us cleave to his preference for concise, effective writing.

Cut the Verbal Fat

In a letter to a twelve-year-old boy, Mark Twain wrote, "I notice you use plain, simple language, short words, and brief sentences. That is the way to write English—it is the modern way and the best way. Stick to it; don't let fluff and flowers and verbosity creep in."

Alas, with most of us, as we grow older, fluff and flowers and verbosity do creep in. Writing today often has too much fat, too little muscle—bulk without strength. Much of what we read these days ranges from slightly flabby to grossly obese. As children we wrote sentences like "See Dick run." As adults, we are more likely to write, "It is imperative that we assiduously observe Richard as he traverses the terrain at an accelerated rate of speed." We gain girth and lose mirth—and so does our prose.

What happens to people's writing in the years between childhood and maturity? For one thing, their reasons for writing change. The child writes for the best of reasons—to tell somebody something that is worth telling. Little Janie Jones wants her friends to know about her dog, Spot. Her only concern is to share her joy that "Spot is the bestest dog in the whole wide world."

Mr. Jones, Janie's dad, also has something worthwhile to write about—his company's new marketing plan, which may or may not be the "bestest" marketing plan in the industry. But his real reason for writing a long memo about the plan is that he wants to be perceived as having had "input" into the plan's development. As he writes, he worries about the impression his writing might make on his colleagues, especially his boss. He chooses his words carefully—the more and the longer, the better. Even if his instinct tells him to write simply, he's afraid to, lest his memo not be taken seriously.

Janie has no such fear. While she uses a simple, clear, unaffected second-grade vocabulary, her dad draws on marketing terms he learned while earning his M.B.A. Relying heavily on the jargon of his business, he throws in a couple of "viable alternatives," a new "set of parameters," and a "plan for prioritization" that "should be implemented *at this point in time*"— the bureaucrat's seventeen-letter word for *now*. When it's done, he has produced a bloated, tedious, pompous piece of writing full of sound and fury signifying very little.

As Janie grows older, her writing gradually becomes more like her dad's—lacking in warmth, sincerity, and directness. She begins to worry about impressing her classmates and teachers, or even Dad, just as Dad worries about impressing his boss. In junior high, her teacher assigns the class a theme about summer vacation and insists that the composition be at least 800 words. This encourages Janie to use 2 or 3 words where one would do the job, to stretch out her composition to the 800-word minimum set by the teacher. So what might have been an interesting, tightly written 500-word piece about a trip to Disney World turns out to be just another example of dull, flabby, padded prose, wheezing away as it lurches uphill.

In addition, Janie and Mr. Jones read so much bloated writing that they start to emulate the style that seems to be the norm. Even if they are fortunate enough to have had good writing instruction in school, they allow hard-learned skills to rust. They lose confidence in their ability to write clearly and convincingly. They underestimate the power and grace of the simple, declarative sentence. To get their points across, they resort to the theory that if one word is good, two words must be twice as good.

Far from contributing to the reader's enlightenment, wordiness enshrouds meaning in a fog of confusion. "Writing improves in direct ratio to the things we can keep out of it that shouldn't be there," advises writing guru William Zinsser. Cutting the fat is probably the quickest and surest way to improve. No matter how solid is your grasp of grammar, punctuation, spelling, and other fundamentals, you cannot write well unless you train yourself to write with fewer words.

British satirist Evelyn Waugh had a low opinion of literary collaboration: "I never could understand how two men can write a book together. To me that's like three people getting together to have a baby." I disagree, having joyfully coauthored seven books. The most recent collaboration was Comma Sense *with John Shore, a wildly imaginative observer and humorist. Working together, we made a book about punctuation that proved the truth of Ecclesiastes 4:9: "Two are better than one." In fact, one plus one added up to way more than two as neither of us alone could have made such a potentially sleep-inducing topic so much fun.*

On Your Marks!

One of life's great oddities is how it's filled with things that don't seem as if they belong together, yet are inextricably joined. Weddings, for instance, and clothes you can barely breathe in. Neckties and having a job. King Kong and Fay Wray. Airplanes and air. Sweet deliciousness and cavities. Bovine flatulence and ozone depletion. Lamb and mint jelly.

Koala bears and weirdly humongous claws. Banana slugs and a rational universe. Menopause and a rational universe. Bill Gates and the future of the universe.

Foremost among things in the world that shouldn't go together but do are Understanding Punctuation and Accruing Personal Power. But it's as true as true gets: If you don't understand punctuation, you can't write right. And if you can't write right, you can't positively influence so much of what's critical to your life.

It's a fact: Good punctuation makes for a good life.

Sure, it seems unfair. But so do lots of things. Parking meters, for instance, seem very unfair. But you can rail against them until Lovely Rita the Meter Maid finally calls for backup—and you'll still end up with a ticket every time you forget to leave the house without a roll of quarters.

Like it or not, writing well—not artistically, not ornately, not floridly, but just competently—really is the difference between being largely able to define your own life and having much of your life defined for you. Writing is, in a word, power. And trying to write even a Post-it note—*much less anything of any substance*—without understanding punctuation is like trying to build a house without nails: It'll look awful, and no one will want to come near it.

Think it's going too far to say that punctuation is the difference between control and chaos, between justice and injustice, between true inner peace and false outer agony? Think that sounds a tad dramatic? Really? Have you ever had the paint on your new car start peeling off in huge flakes? Ever had a rabid boss ruin your life? Ever yearned for someone of the opposite sex to fall heels over head in love with you?

You see the point: If you want to impress that special gal or fella, use your blotchy new car to run over your rabid boss.

No, the *real* point is: Knowing how to write clear, succinct, and, if need be, charming letters, notes, and e-mails is one extremely dependable way to persuade people to start thinking about matters in precisely the way you would prefer them to.

It's how you get your car repainted for free. It's how you (eventually) get your loser boss fired. It's how you get that gal or fella to lie awake nights wondering why they never learned how to punctuate, so that they could scribe communiqués as enticing as yours.

Just look at the difference between these two love notes:

> My Dear Pat,
>
> The dinner we shared the other night—it was absolutely lovely! Not in my wildest dreams could I ever imagine anyone as perfect as you are. Could you—if only for a moment—think of our being together forever? What a cruel joke to have you come into my life only to leave again; it would be heaven denied. The possibility of seeing you again makes me giddy with joy. I face the time we are apart with great sadness.
>
> John
>
>
> P.S. I would like to tell you that I love you. I can't stop thinking that you are one of the prettiest women on earth.

My *Dear,*

Pat the dinner we shared the other night. It was absolutely lovely—not! In my wildest dreams, could I ever imagine anyone? As perfect as you are, could you—if only for a moment—think? Of our being together forever: what a cruel joke! To have you come into my life only to leave again: It would be heaven! Denied the possibility of seeing you again makes me giddy. With joy I face the time we are apart.

With great "sadness,"

John

P.S. I would like to tell you that I love you. I can't. Stop thinking that you are one of the prettiest women on earth.

You see the difference punctuation makes? The first letter is a clear (albeit clunky) profession of undying affection; the second is sure to sweep Pat *onto* her feet. The only thing separating one document from the other is, of course, punctuation.

Never forget: Punctuation can mean the difference between a second date and a restraining order.

And never forget the single Great Truth about Punctuation: If you fail to master its art and craft, your life will be littered with the shards of broken dreams. Or, less melodramatically, your life will be littered with the shards of broken beer bottles, the contents of which you have drunk to avoid thinking about your dead-end job.

There may be no better way to acquire more power in one fell swoosh than to master the fundamentals of punctuation and become a power pack of punctuational potency. Believe it now, or believe it when you find a bunch of people standing around the water cooler at work laughing at one of your memos. (The cruel fact about punctuation, remember, is that a person doesn't have to know how to use it in order to know, right away, when someone *else* has botched it beyond respectability.)

"Your report, Ms. Jones, was dismal; I cannot imagine how you ever came to work here." That's power. "Your report Ms. Jones was dismal I cannot imagine. how you ever came to work here?" is . . . so not.

The power's in the punctuation, baby.

The fact is that the average person can't punctuate their way out of "See Spot run." Lost in a sea of punctuational possibilities, they come up with "See? Spot run!" or "See Spot! Run!" or "See, Spot has the runs!" This doesn't make them bad people, of course, or spectacularly dense people, or anything like that. It makes them people who don't know how to punctuate. That there are so many of them out there is absolutely wonderful news for you: It means that people who *can* punctuate stand out like Thinking Gods.

Thinking Gods!

Or, you know: just a normal person who writes well.

The
Joys of
Lex

What is there about words that makes a language person love them so? There are probably as many answers as there are logophiles. How do we love thee, language? Let me count the ways.

Confessions of a Verbivore

One day I found myself chatting with Mrs. Marilyn Frazier's class of sixth-grade students at Broken Ground School in Concord, New Hampshire, about the joys of language and the challenges of the writing life. During the question-and-answer session that followed, one of the boys in the class asked me, "Mr. Lederer, where do you get your ideas for your books?"

Ever since I became a writer, I had found that question to be the most difficult to answer, and I had only recently come up with an analogy that I thought would satisfy both my audience and me. Pouncing on the opportunity to unveil my spanking-new explanation for the first time, I countered with "Where does the spider get its web?"

The idea, of course, was that the spider is not aware of how it spins out intricate and beautiful patterns with the silky material that is simply a natural part of itself. Asking a writer to account for the genesis of his or her ideas is as futile as asking a spider to explain the source of its web and the method of its construction.

So when the young man asked his question, I replied, "Where does the spider get its web?"

He shot right back, "From its butt!"

Since that visit, I've checked out the boy's assertion, and, sure enough, spiders do produce their silk from glands located in their posteriors. The glands open through the tiny spinnerets located at the hind end of the abdomen. Well, it may be that for lo these many years I've been talking and writing through my butt, but that doesn't stop me from being a self-confessed and unrepentant verbivore.

Carnivores eat flesh and meat; piscivores eat fish; herbivores consume plants and vegetables; verbivores devour words. I am such a creature. My whole life I have feasted on words—ogled their appetizing shapes, colors, and textures; swished them around in my mouth; lingered over their many tastes; let their juices run down my chin. During my adventures as a fly-by-the-roof-of-the-mouth, user-friendly wizard of idiom, I have met thousands of other wordaholics, logolepts, and verbivores—folks who also eat their words.

Some word-struck people are intrigued by the birth and life of words. They become enthusiastic, ebullient, and enchanted when they discover that *enthusiastic* literally means "possessed by a god," *ebullient* "boiling over, spouting out," and *enchanted* "singing a magic song." They are rendered starry-eyed by the insight that *disaster* (*dis-aster*) literally means *"ill-starred"* and intoxicated by the information that *intoxicated* has poison in its heart. They love the fact that *amateur* is cobbled from the very first verb that all students of Latin learn—*amo*: "I love."

Wordsters of etymological persuasion love to track down the origins of phrases. Take "sitting in the catbird seat." The expression was popularized by Red Barber, the colorful broadcaster for the Brooklyn Dodgers, who also spread the likes of "tearing up the pea patch" and *rhubarb*, used to mean "an argument on a baseball diamond." The Mississippi-born Barber once explained that "sitting in the catbird seat" was a Southern expression for which he had literally paid. In a stud poker game Barber continually bluffed with a weak hand until he lost to an opponent who met every raise. According to Red, the winner, who held an ace showing and an ace in the hole, said, "Thanks for all those raises. From the start, I was sitting in the catbird seat."

The catbird commands a good view from its lofty perch, but so do many other birds. My reading of ornithology books reveals that the catbird does not usually sit high up in branches, where it could get the best view, but rather lurks half-hidden in shrubbery. What's so special about the catbird and its vantage point? Intrepid bird-watchers, word-botchers, and phrase-hunters will never rest until they track down the answer.

Then there's the breed of logophile who enjoys trying to

turn the brier patch of pronoun cases, subject-verb agreement, sequence of tenses, and the indicative and subjunctive moods into a manageable garden of delight. Such devotees of correct usage often explore the nuances of confusing word pairs—*take* versus *bring* (you take out the garbage; you bring in the newspaper), *podium* versus *lectern* (you stand on a podium; you stand behind a lectern), and *comprise* versus *compose* (they're antonyms, not synonyms: the large comprises the small; the small composes the large).

Language derives from *lingua*, "tongue," so it is no surprise that many verbivores care deeply about the pronunciation of words. The sounding *noo-kyuh-lur* has received much notoriety because a number of presidents from Dwight David Eisenhower to George W. Bush have spoken the word that way. A great many people riding our fair planet simply cannot hear the difference between *noo-kyuh-lur* and *noo-klee-uhr*.

Noo-kyuh-lur is an example of metathesis, the transposition of internal sounds, as in *ree-luh-tur* for *realtor*, *joo-luh-ree* for *jewelry*, *lahr-niks* for *larynx*, and, more subtly, *cumf-ter-bull* for *comfortable*. But while the metathesis *cumf-ter-bull* (in which the *er* and the *t* have been transposed) is fully acceptable and entrenched in our language, cultivated speakers generally consider *noo-kyuh-lur*, *ree-lah-tur*, and their ilk atrocities. *The San Diego Union-Tribune* recently polled its readers to find out the grammar and pronunciation abuses that most seismically yanked their chains and rattled their cages. *Noo-kyuh-lur* was the crime against English mentioned by the greatest number of respondents. *Noo-kyuh-lur* made them go ballistic, even *noo-klee-ur.* Despite its proliferation, *noo-kyuh-lur* has failed to gain respectability. *Noo-kyuh-lur* may be a sad fact of life, but resistance to it is hardly a lost cause. Although we hear it from some prominent people, it remains a much-derided aberration.

Among my favorite wordmongers are those who prowl the lunatic fringes of language—*lunatic* because the ancients believed that prolonged exposure to the moon (Latin *luna*) rendered one moonstruck, or daft. These recreational word-players delight in how we English users are constantly standing meaning on its head, as in these familiar phrases about our bodies:

Watch your head

We keep seeing this sign on low doorways, but we haven't figured out how to follow the instructions. Trying to watch your head is like trying to bite your teeth.

Put your best foot forward

Now let's see. . . . We have a good foot and a better foot, but we don't have a third—and best—foot.

Keep a stiff upper lip

When we are disappointed or afraid, which lip do we try to control? The lower lip, of course, is the one we are trying to keep from quivering.

I'm speaking tongue in cheek

So how can anyone understand you?

Skinny

If *fatty* means "full of fat," shouldn't *skinny* mean "full of skin"?

They do things behind my back

You want they should do things in front of your back?

They did it ass backwards

What's wrong with that? We do *everything* ass backwards.

Still another denomination of verbivore sees words as collections of letters to be juggled, shuffled, and flipped. Lovers of logology—the art and craft of letter play—are spellbound by the fact that TWENTY-NINE is spelled with straight letters made of straight lines only—twenty-nine of them, to be exact—and that *ambidextrous* is alphabetically ambidextrous. Its left half, Ambide, uses letters from the left half of the alphabet, and its right half, *xtrous*, uses letters from the right half of the alphabet.

Inspired by the word *bookkeeper*, with its three consecutive pairs of double letters, these logologists fantasize about a biologist who helps maintain raccoon habitats: *a raccoon nook keeper*—six consecutive sets of double letters—and another biologist who studies the liquid secreted by chickadee eggs. They call this scientist a *chickadee egg gooologist*—and into the world are born three consecutive pairs of triple letters!

Finally, there are the legions of pundits, punheads, and pun pals who tell of the Buddhist who said to the hot dog vendor, "Make me one with everything." That's the same Buddhist who never took Novocain when he had teeth extracted because he wished to transcend dental medication. These punderful verbivores become even bigger hot dogs when they tell about Charlemagne, who mustered his Franks and set out with great relish to assault and pepper the Saracens, but he couldn't catch up. (Frankly, I never sausage a pun. It's the wurst!)

Incorrigible pun-gent that I am (don't incorrige me!), I love sharpening my pun cells for the moment when everything comes together to form an incisive and contextual prey on words:

During my first tour of our San Diego Wild Animal Park, I went to an area where giraffes lean forward over a parapet and accept food from visitors. I suggested to the keeper that the area be named Giraffic Park. Watching an Imax film about volcanoes from Fiji to Hawaii, I noted the title, *Ring of Fire*, turned to my long-suffering wife, and commented, "They've missed the best title for this movie—*Ash from a Hole in the Ground*." At an airport security area I removed my shoes and then placed them in one of the small tubs because my size fourteens are supported by large steel shanks that unfailingly set bells a ringing. When, after a long wait, the attendant finally returned my shoes, I thanked her for "the shoe shank redemption." I love pushing the envelope of language, even if it causes those around me to be out of sorts and go postal.

At rare times, all these verbivorous elements come together in a single word. Has there ever been another word as human as *usher*? In sound and meaning it is not a paragon among words, but it accommodates the full spectrum of humankind. Words and people have always hung around together, and within the brief compass of the five letters in *usher*, we find the pronouns *us, she, he*, and *her*. Like humanity, *usher* has a long history, going all the way back to the Latin *ostium*, "door," related to *os*, "mouth," because a door was likened to the mouth of a building. So there again is that iron link between things and human beings.

Usher winkingly reminds us that all words are created by people and that language unfailingly reflects the fearful asymmetry of our kind. Thus, even though writers write, bakers bake, hunters hunt, preachers preach, and teachers teach, grocers don't groce, butchers don't butch, carpenters don't carpent, milliners don't millin, haberdashers don't haberdash—and ushers don't ush.

I am heels over head in love with language. When I say *heels over head*, rather than *head over heels*, I am not two letters short of a complete alphabet or a syllable short of a coherent statement. *Head over heels* is the normal position, sort of like doing things ass backwards, which is the way we do everything.

I don't know about you, but when I flip over something, my heels are over my head.

When I say *language*, I mean by and large that glorious, uproarious, notorious, outrageous, contagious, courageous, stupendous, tremendous, end-over-endous adventure we call the English language. That's because in matters verbal I am unabashedly lexist. Just as many would say that, among many other things, the Italians do food well and that, among their many other accomplishments, the French do style and fashion well, I believe that we English speakers and writers do language especially well. One might say that we do it lexicellently.

"Give me a lever long enough and a prop strong enough," wrote the ancient Greek mathematician and inventor Archimedes, "and I can single-handedly move the world." Riposted the Polish writer Joseph Conrad more than two millennia later, "Do not talk to me of Archimedes' lever. He was an absent-minded man with a mathematical imagination. Give me the right word and the right accent, and I will move the world." The words you use may indeed help you to lift your life. Studies over many decades have shown that a wide-ranging, powerful vocabulary is directly linked to career advancement, to financial well-being, and even to social success. Life itself is richer the more words you have to describe it and to figure it out.

Add Wealth to Your Vocabulary

During the early years of space exploration, NASA scientist Wernher Von Braun gave many speeches on the wonders and promises of rocketry and space flight. After one of his luncheon talks, Von Braun found himself clinking cock-tail glasses with an adoring woman from the audience.

"Dr. Von Braun," the woman gushed, "I just loved your speech, and I found it of absolutely infinitesimal value!"

"Well then," Von Braun gulped, "I guess I'll have to pub-lish it posthumously."

"Oh, yes," the woman came right back. "And the sooner the better!"

Now *there* was someone who needed to gain greater con-trol over her vocabulary. But, realizing the power that words confer on our lives, don't we all wish that we could build a bet-ter vocabulary?

Justice Oliver Wendell Holmes once declared that "lan-guage is the skin of living thought." Holmes recognized that just as our skin bounds and encloses our body, so does our vo-cabulary bound and enclose our mental life.

Suppose, for example, you wish to describe something of great size. You can haul out those two old standbys *big* and *large*. But if you possess an extensive vocabulary, you can press into service an army of more powerful and muscular adjec-tives: *tremendous, immense, enormous, huge, vast,* or *gigantic.*

If, in addition to size, you wish to convey the suggestion of solidity and immovability, you can use words such as *massive, bulky, unwieldy, jumbo, elephantine,* and *mountainous.* If you want to create an image of clumsiness, you can call into service the likes of *lumbering* and *ponderous. Hulking, looming,* and *monstrous* add a sense of threat to the impression of size, while *mighty, towering,* and *colossal* indicate that the size inspires awe.

It's a matter of simple mathematics: The more words you know, the more choices you can make; the more choices you can make, the more accurate, vivid, and varied your speaking and writing will be.

Here are five methods you can use to enrich your vocabulary and, as a result, your ability to communicate:

1. **Read! Read! Read!** When you were a child learning to speak, you seized each word as if it were a shiny toy. This is how you learned your language, and this is how you can expand your word stock.

   The best way to learn new words is through reading. Read for pleasure. Read for information. Read everything you can find on any subject that interests you. Read short stories. Read novels. Read nonfiction. Read newspapers. Read magazines. Soak up words like a sponge. The more words you read, the more words you will know. The more words you know, the better you will be able to communicate—and think.

2. **Infer meaning from context.** There is another reason why reading is an effective way to grow vocabulary. A word that stands by itself offers fewer clues to its meaning than does a word that is related by sense to other words in a sentence or paragraph. These surrounding words make up the context (from Latin *contextere*, "to weave together") in which the unknown word is used.

Detectives use clues to help them make deductions and solve cases. You can become a word detective and deduce the meaning of an unknown word by taking into account the words that surround it and the situation being talked or written about.

Here are four ways that you can discover the meaning of a new word from its setting.

a. **Situation.** "Many agricultural experts say that if properly harvested, the arable lands of Ethiopia and Sudan could feed most of the continent." *Arable* means: _____.

b. **Examples and illustrations.** "Critic, essayist, historian, travel writer, diarist, Edmund Wilson was a protean man of letters, one of his era's representative figures." *Protean* means: _____.

c. **Restatement.** One of our finest poets, at the height of his power, he brings together and unifies tendencies that might have divided opposing poets into separate elements." *Unifies* means: _____.

d. **Contrast.** "The advent of television eventually swept away the huge, grandly ornate movie palaces of the 1920s and left in their place small, utterly functional, faceless theaters." *Ornate* means: _____.

(*answers:* a. capable of being farmed b. displaying great variety c. joins together separate elements d. elaborate, richly decorated)

3. **Dig down to the roots.** Words and people have a lot in common. Like people, words are born, grow up, get married, have children, and even die. And, like people, words come in families—big and beautiful families. A word family is a cluster of words that are related because they contain the same root; a root is a basic building block of language from which a variety of related words are formed. You can expand your vocabulary by digging down to the roots of an unfamiliar word and identifying the meanings of those roots.

    For example, knowing that the roots *scribe* and *script* mean "write" will help you to deduce the meanings of a prolific clan of words, including *ascribe, conscript, describe, inscribe, manuscript, nondescript, postscript, prescribe, proscribe, scribble, scripture,* and *transcribe*. For another example, once you know that *dic* and *dict* are roots that mean "speak or say," you possess a key that unlocks the meanings of dozens of related words, including *abdicate, benediction, contradict, dedicate, dictator, Dictaphone, dictionary, dictum, edict, indicate, indict, interdict, malediction, predict, syndicate, valedictory, verdict, vindicate,* and *vindictive*.

    Suppose that you encounter the word *antipathy* in speech or writing. From words like *antiwar* and *antifreeze* you can infer that the root *anti-* means "against," and from words like *sympathy* and *apathy* that *path* is a root that means "feeling." From such insights it is but a short leap to deduce that *antipathy* means "feeling against something." This process of rooting out illustrates the old saying "It's hard by the yard but a cinch by the inch."

You can expand your verbal powers by learning to look an unfamiliar word squarely in the eye and asking, "What are the roots in the word, and what do they mean?" Here are twenty word parts descended from either Latin or Greek, each followed by three words containing each root. From the meanings of the clue words, deduce the meaning of each root, as in PHON—microphone, phonics, telephone = *sound:*

1. AUTO—autobiography, autograph, automation = _____
2. CHRON—chronic, chronology, synchronize = _____
3. CULP—culpable, culprit, exculpate = _____
4. EU—eugenics, eulogy, euphemism = _____
5. GREG—congregation, gregarious, segregate = _____
6. LOQU—eloquent, loquacious, soliloquy = _____
7. MAGN—magnanimous, magnify, magnitude = _____
8. NOV—innovation, novelty, renovate = _____

9. OMNI—omnipotent, omniscient, omnivorous = _____

10. PHIL—bibliophile, philanthropy, philology = _____

11. SOL—isolate, soliloquy, solitary = _____

12. SOPH—philosopher, sophistication, sophomore = _____

13. TELE—telegraph, telephone, television = _____

14. TEN—tenacious, tenure, untenable = _____

15. TRACT—extract, intractable, tractor = _____

16. VAC—evacuate, vacation, vacuum = _____

17. VERT—convert, introvert, vertigo = _____

18. VIV—survivor, vivacious, vivid = _____

19. VOC—invoke, vocal, vociferous = _____

20. VOL—malevolent, volition, voluntary = _____

(*answers:* 1. self 2. time 3. blame 4. good 5. kind, species 6. speak 7. large 8. new 9. all 10. love 11. alone 12. wise, wisdom 13. far away 14. hold 15. pull 16. empty 17. turn 18. life, lively 19. call, voice 20. wish)

4. **Get the dictionary habit.** Mark Twain once wrote, "A dictionary is the most awe-inspiring of all books; it knows so much. It has gone around the sun, and spied out everything and lit it up." The practice of using the dictionary is essential in acquiring a mighty and versatile vocabulary. Keep an

up-to-date dictionary by your side when you read. Whenever you run across a word that you are not sure of, look it up—a process that will probably take you no more than thirty seconds. Then record the word and its meaning on your private word list.

5. **Use your new words.** As soon as you have captured a new word in your mind, use it in conversation or writing. When you see a new word in your own handwriting, you are more likely to remember it.

Try using at least one new word each day. Tell your parents how much you *venerate* them. Compliment your children on their *altruism* when they stoop to share the remote with you. Congratulate your business associates on their *enthralling* and *edifying* presentation. Explain to Tabby that she shouldn't be so *intractable* about consuming her cat food.

And remind yourself not to *procrastinate* about acquiring and using new words. Make vocabulary growth a lifelong adventure. You're never too old to learn, and that includes learning vocabulary. In the process, you will expand your thoughts and your feelings, your speaking, your reading, and your writing—everything that makes up you.

The great American dictionary maker Noah Webster once asked Basil Hall, a naval officer from England, why he considered all American coinages unworthy. "Because," Captain Hall replied, with typical British assurance, "there are enough words already." Two centuries after that exchange we know that there are never enough words.

Words, Words, Words

How many words are there in English? This apparently simple question turns out to be surprisingly complicated. The answer partly depends on what you count as English words and where you go looking for them.

One place, of course, is "the dictionary." In the United States, Noah Webster's 1806 dictionary included about 37,000 words, but his 1826 edition contained about 70,000. *The Century Dictionary*, which appeared in 1889, held about 200,000, and by 1911 the editors found it necessary to add 100,000 more. Merriam-Webster's *Third New International Dictionary*, published in 1961, lists more than 450,000 words and the *Oxford English Dictionary* some 616,500. One thing is certain:

Modern English has the largest and richest word hoard of any human language ever known.

But no one can be sure how many words there are in English. As good as our lexicographers are at catching and exhibiting words, no dictionary can be complete. There are well over a million organic and inorganic chemical compounds, each with its own distinctive name, along with several million insects that have been named, with millions more flying or crawling around yet unlabeled. In fact, three-quarters of our words belong to specialized fields such as medicine, psychology, and technology or to trade jargons. Dictionaries for general use simply have no room for most of these words.

In addition, the English language grows at a rate of about 1,000 words each year. Words such as *cybrarian* and *metrosexual* continuously spring up. These neophytes are so hot and so new that they are not enshrined in many dictionaries, but they do exist as words.

Among the 0.5 million words that repose in our biggest, fattest American dictionaries, how many belong to the average speaker? To answer this question, we must distinguish between two kinds of vocabulary: those words we recognize or recall, and those we actually use. The average person possesses a vocabulary of 10–20,000 words but actively uses only a small fraction of these, the others being recognition or recall vocabulary. In fact, a number of linguists claim that 9 words make up 25 percent of our speech *the, of, and, a, to, in, it, for,* and *he.*

According to language scholars, 34 more words make up another 25 percent, so that 43 words make up 50 percent of our speech. These 34 words are all one-syllable and include *have, I, they, with, not, she, on, at, this,* and *by.* A recent statistical study of U.S. telephone speech revealed that 737 words make up 96 percent of all conversations.

A literate adult may recognize 60,000 or more words, the most learned of us 100,000. The surprising fact remains that the most articulate verbivore interacts with only one-fifth of the total official word stock and actually employs a far smaller fraction. The most verbal of us are still semiliterate.

The increasing complexity of society and the rapid growth of technology have led to an explosion in the number of words at our disposal. More new words were added to English between 1850 and 1950 in the field of chemistry alone than Old English acquired from all sources in five hundred years.

The accelerating growth of English will increase the gap between the individual's vocabulary and the total number of words in the language. Our language is a classic case of conspicuous consumption—or perhaps we should say nonconsumption because so many words remain unemployed. Fortunately, we seldom miss the words we never use and can get along without them. But we should count our linguistic blessings. In language, an embarrassment of wealth is preferable to an embarrassment of poverty.

I invite you, O illecebrous, impigrous, isangelous, leg-giadrous, peramene, swasivious, viscerotonic reader (trust me that I am paying you compliments), to share the pleasures of exhuming weird and wonderful words from forgotten graves. In the process of such etymological excavation, you'll find that there are more words in our English lexicon than are dreamt of in your philosophies.

Weird Words

When I was a lad, I played with those small winged thingamabobs that grow on—and contain the seeds of—maple trees. I glued them to my nose and watched them spin like pinwheels when I tossed them into the wind. Only as a grown-up did I discover that these organic whatchamacallits do have a name—*samara*. So do the uglifying fleshy growth on a turkey's face—a *wattle*—and the heavy flaps on the sides of the mouths of some dogs—*flews*. So do all sorts of human body parts that you never thought had names—*canthus, cerumen, frenulum, opisthenar, philtrum, thenar, tragus, uvula,* and *vomer.*

Name givers of the past have designated the half-smoked plug of tobacco in a pipe bowl as *dottle*, the decaying matter on a forest floor as *duff*, the holder for a paper-cone coffee cup the *zarf*, and the slit made when one starts to saw a piece of wood as the *kerf*.

Ever since Adam assigned names to all the animals, we human beings have managed to come up with labels for almost everything on this planet—and beyond. Many of these names are so obscure that no one except dictionary editors knows them. The rest of us are reduced to referring to these things with words that mean "that object I don't know the name for." We have even managed to come up with more than thirty ways of signifying that for which we don't have a name, including *curwhibble*, *doohickey*, *gigamaree*, *thingumajog*, and *whatchamacallit*. Plumbing the depths of our abounding English vocabulary provides a remedy for that tongue-tangled state. Weird words help us to fill in the semantic holes of all those doohickeys and whatchamacallits and brush bursting color onto the patches of blank in our picture of the world.

According to the Mayan sacred book Popol Vuh, after the Creators had made the earth, carved it with mountains, valleys, and rivers, and covered it with vegetation, they formed the animals who would be guardians of the plant world and who would praise the Makers' names:

"Speak, then, our names, praise us, your mother, your father. Invoke, then, Huracan, Chipi-Caculha, the Heart of Heaven, the Heart of Earth, the Creator, the

Maker, the Forefathers. Speak, invoke us, adore us." But the animals only hissed and screamed and cackled. They were unable to make words, and each screamed in a different way. When the Creator and the Maker saw that it was impossible for them to talk to each other, they said: "It is impossible for them to say the names of us, their Creators and Makers. This is not well." As a punishment, the birds and animals were condemned to be eaten and sacrificed by others, and the Creators set out to make another creature who would be able to call their names and speak their praises. This creature was man and woman.

The human passion and power to name everything are nowhere better demonstrated than in our ability to label almost everything we encounter. Through the wabe of our word-bethumped English-language gyre and gimble as many as two million words—the most gargantuan vocabulary by far in the history of humankind. Such a wealth of words creates a case of inconspicuous nonconsumption. Thousands of vibrant, but no longer vibrating, English words lie unused in the arcane crannies of huge or obscure dictionaries and end up buried in the boneyards of obsolescence.

You probably don't know single words can describe the rosy light of dawn, the cooing of doves, the art of writing in the dark, or (in the manner of Georges Simenon and Isaac Asimov) the act of continuous writing, but there is a word for each concept—*rosicler*, *roucoulement*, *scoteography*, and *scriptitation*.

These verbal treasures were long ago untimely ripped from our vocabularies and deserve another chance to live. Are you, like me, a water drinker and booze-shunner? Then you are, in a word, an aquabib. Do you, like Shaquille O'Neal and me, have large feet? You are, in another word, scipodous. Perhaps Macbeth and his henpecking, buzzard-battering lady would have lived and ended their lives less bloodily if they had known that they were both dretched ("troubled in sleep") by sanguinolency ("addiction to bloodshed").

Weird words confer superb opportunities to insult your enemies with inventive invective and impious impunity. By creatively combining disparaging archaisms, you can brand your nemesis a badot cumber-ground ("silly person who takes up space"), a furciferous lordswike ("rascally traitor"), a balatronic hoddypeak ("buffoonlike blockhead"), a trichechine jollux ("walruslike fat person"), a sclestious volpone ("wicked schemer"), a testudineous windlestraw ("slow-moving, tall, unhealthy-looking person"), a scolecophagous stadafor ("worm-eating impostor"), a drumbling gilly-gaupus ("sluggish fool"), and a roinish and uliginous drazel ("scabby, slimy slut")!

Remembrance of words past also raises the art of the euphemism to its loftiest stratum. That's not a double chin you sport, it's a choller. If you are fixated on the care and maintenance of your hair, you are not narcissistic; you are, more mysteriously and less judgmentally, philocomal. If you have a friend who used to share your interests but—weep weep, sob sob, snort snort—no longer does, he or she evidences ageustia, the loss of the sense of taste. If your relatives are bugging you about your state of singlehood, explain that you are happy to be agamous, and they may come to share your joy.

Add the benefit of the crackling logophony of the many dearly departed words that tingle around the tongue and ricochet off the teeth and palate. I'll not define these ear-rinsing words; simply allow yourself to merge with the collide-o-scope of their sounds: *Bogglish. Camstairy. Flambuginous. Impluvious. Infrendiate. Jirble. Kakistocracy. Rixation. Sardoodledom. Whistness. Winx. Zizany.*

Trust me: It's not inaniloquent morology ("babbling foolishness") and balbutiating galimatias ("stuttering nonsene") driveling from my fingertips massaging the keyboard when I tell you that lost words demonstrate that there are lots of things and ideas in the universe that actually do have names even though hardly anybody knows them. Spotted owls, snail darters, and whales are not the only treasures on our endangered list these days. Scores of our most colorful and precise words are on the verge of extinction after generations of service. Fortunately, these specimens of logodiversity find refuge and rejuvenation in wild-word sanctuaries. The lexicographers who rescue weird words are not harmless drudges. Rather, they remind us of the unbounded generativity of our word-happy English language.

On my public radio show, A Way with Words, *we find that many of the bread-and-butter questions from our callers are about grammar and usage: "Does none take a singular or a plural verb?" "Is irregardless a word?" "Isn't the pronoun myself being overused these days?" People want to know what's right and what's wrong. For years such inquiries have helped to shape my philosophy about correctness in speech and writing. Here's where my thinking is now.*

Conan the Grammarian

Call me Conan the Grammarian: Undangler of Participles, Destroyer of Gratuitous Apostrophes, Protector of Pronoun Cases. I know that I am not alone in this reaction. Riding this planet are millions of us for whom the maintenance of standard usage is as important as preserving our environment.

I am not Conan the Unsplitter of Split Infinitives, the Terminator of Terminal Prepositions. The injunctions against cleft infinitives and terminal prepositions are completely bogus. Such proclamations exist as sheer rumor and gossip. They are never enshrined in reputable usage manuals.

I own a Ph.D. in linguistics, the scientific study of language, so I'm supposed to see language change as neither good nor bad but as natural evolution. I am aware that English is a living language. Like a tree, language sheds its leaves and grows new ones so that it may live on. But to recognize the reality of and the need for change does not mean that we must accept the mindless permissiveness that pervades the use of English in our society.

I consider myself to be a compassionate prescriptivist. I understand that—and here comes a second metaphor—standard usage is written on the sand. But although that sand may one day erode or blow away, at any moment in history the rules of usage are written in the collective consciousness of caring and careful users of our language. Years from now "Me and Mary have a ball with language" and "The book is laying on the table" may be Standard English, but they are not now.

I truly believe that to reap the full fruits of American civilization (*hmmm*, a third metaphor), one must be in control of the dialect we call Standard English, the dialect that most books and business reports are written in and most broadcasts are broadcast in.

There are those who contend, "Who cares how you say or write something as long as people understand you?" This is like saying, "Who cares what clothing you wear, as long as it keeps you warm and covers your nakedness?" But clothing does more than provide warmth and cover, just as language does more than transfer ideas. The sensible man or woman knows when to wear a business suit and when to wear a T-shirt and shorts, when to wear a tuxedo and when to wear a flannel shirt and dungarees. So that's my fifth metaphor/analogy: Both clothing and language make statements about the wearer and the user.

Thus, in an effort to make the world a better place, I cleave to Lederer's Three Rules of Correcting Others:

1. Are you right?
2. Will it make a difference?
3. If conditions 1. and 2. are met, do the correcting in private.

I visit my doctor, and his nurse instructs me to "lay down on the table." I am excruciatingly aware that millions of Americans seem unable to distinguish between *lie*, an intransitive verb that means "repose," and *lay*, a transitive verb that means "put." They do not grasp that once they're done laying a book on the table, it lies—not lays—there. Pardon the fowl language, but a hen on its back is lying; a hen on its stomach may be laying—an egg.

But enough (please don't ask me to quantify when enough is "enough") of us Standard English speakers and writers adhere to that distinction that I feel that I'm right about enforcing it in reasonably formal situations. And in the case of the nurse, who's probably misusing *lay* many times each day and could lose the doctor business, I feel that my interposition will make a difference. So, with a smile, not a sneer, I correct her in the privacy of the examining room and hope that she won't seek revenge on me by ordering up three successive prostate probes.

I'm speaking before a group, and the master of ceremonies asks me if I want to place my notes "on the podium." I think to myself, "How could I stoop so low?", but I do not correct my host. It's true that etymologically a *lectern* (from the Latin *legere*, "to read") is the slant-topped desk, while a *podium* (from the Greek *podion*, "foot") is the small base on which the speaker stands, but my personal polls show that more than 90 percent of the U.S. population (and this includes my surveys of English teachers) uses *podium* to stand for either item of furniture. So I hold my tongue.

I know that *anxious* and *eager* have both been used for centuries to mean "characterized by anxiety." But enough of us Standard English users distinguish between "I'm eager to meet you" (happy anticipation) and "I'm anxious about meeting you" (evincing anxiety) that I feel urges to correct those who say or write, "I'm anxious to meet you." On the other hand, so few of us cleave to the belief that something that encourages health is *healthful* and makes us *healthy* that I do not don my Conan the Grammarian cape for that battle. In fact, I congratulate the folks who came up with the name Healthy Choice for the frozen-food line. They're selling a lot more packages than if they'd named the product Healthful Choice.

Should we feel badly about "I feel badly"? Although "I feel badly that I let you down" represents an admirable attempt to differentiate physical ill-being ("I feel bad") from emotional ill-being ("I feel badly"), much in the manner of "I feel good" versus "I feel well," "feel badly" has been criticized for about a century.

When I ask the offended why they object, their voices slip into the tonal groove that the century-old explanation has worn for itself: "If you feel badly, your fingertips must be sandpapered or Novocained, or you're wearing thick gloves." *Har har*—but for a great number of people this disapproval is very real.

When I attempt to explain to the finger-waggers that the *badly* in *feel badly* is not an adverb but an adjective, in the manner of *costly, elderly, friendly, kindly, sickly,* and more than a hundred other adjectives that wag *–ly* tails, they still feel strongly (ahem!) that *feel badly* is somehow wrongheaded. So at this juncture in our history, to avoid the disapproval of others, I recommend that you feel bad, not badly.

Do students graduate from an institution, or do they graduate that institution? Well, an institution graduates its students. Therefore, the most logical way to speak and write about an awarding of diplomas is "I was graduated from Bilgewater State in 1968," and that passive construction was the traditional idiom from the sixteenth century into the nineteenth century.

Gradually "I graduated from" came in and supplanted "I was graduated from," except in highly formal statements, such as wedding announcements: "Born and raised in Philadelphia, the groom was graduated from the University of Pennsylvania." Nowadays many Americans, especially younger ones, like to drop prepositions and particle verbs and say, "Let's hang," "Can you deal?", "Don't cave." Thus, there is pressure to say and write, "I graduated Bilgewater State in 1968." Nonetheless, "I graduated *from*" remains the standard idiom—for now—and I, Conan the Grammarian, stoutly defend it.

Part of being a compassionate corrector is knowing when *not* to correct even a blatant boo-boo. Almost thirty years ago, my thirteen-year-old son brought home a sign he had lovingly crafted in junior high school wood shop. It read, "The Lederer's." You see this apostrophe catastrophe in front of houses and on mailboxes everywhere: "The Smith's," "The Gump's." These "prepostrophes" are distressing signs of our times. Which Smith? Which Gump? Here we have an atrocity of both case and number in one felonious swoop.

Who lives in the house? The Smiths. The Gumps. The Lederers. That's what the signs should say. It's really nobody else's business whether the Smiths, the Gumps, or the Lederers own their domiciles. All we need know is that the Smiths, the Gumps, and the Lederers reside there. If you must announce possession, place the apostrophe after the plural: The Smiths'. The Gumps'. The Lederers'.

At that time, I didn't tell my son that he was a victim of a nationwide conspiracy of junior high school shop teachers dedicated to spreading apostrophe catastrophe throughout our land. You see, I'm a compassionate corrector.

The sign still sits in front of our home, and I still haven't told my son, who's now forty-two Why? I love my boy, and he still comes to visit.

Games are a natural part of my writing because enjoyment and instruction are inspiring team teachers. When a reader performs aerobics of the mind and push-ups of the brain to explore a linguistic concept, language play becomes language power. The game you're about to learn is a favorite of mine because my three children were brought up playing endless rounds of it during long car trips. I'm convinced that all those hours of juggling sounds and definitions made them more verbivorous adults. Howard's DVDs are the most widely watched of all instructional poker products. Annie and Katy have each written bestselling memoirs. You could say that my children are engaged in a scribbling rivalry.

Inky Pinky

What do you get when you dip your little finger into a bottle of writing fluid? An inky pinky.

Looking for an entertaining way to sharpen both your ear for rhyme and your skill in defining words? Try the Inky Pinky game. In Inky Pinky, the first player offers a concise, clear definition, and the second player must translate that definition into two words that rhyme. The first player must also indicate the number of syllables in each word by saying, "Ink Pink" for one-syllable words, "Inky Pinky" for two-syllable words, and so on.

To warm up for the challenge, consider the following examples:

> **DEFINITION:** an uncontrollable youngster.
> *Ink Pink.*
> **ANSWER:** wild child.
> **DEFINITION:** a dumb little boy with a bow and
> arrow. *Inky Pinky.*
> **ANSWER:** stupid cupid.
> **DEFINITION:** yearly handbook. *Inky Pinky.*
> **ANSWER:** an annual manual.

Now that the chalk talk is over, translate the following lists of definitions into rhyming pairs, using the headings as clues to the number of syllables in each word. For more fun, create your own definitions and challenge your family and friends to discover the rhymed answers.

★ Ink Pink ★

1. *inexpensive land vehicle*
2. *short poetry*
3. *strange facial hair*
4. *meat robber*
5. *large dried fruit*
6. *contemptible sign of happiness*
7. *crack in a safe*

8. dock for shorties
9. pale long-necked bird
10. shining armor-wearer
11. crazy flatboat
12. intelligent pointed missile
13. bad smell in a ditch
14. bad-tempered monarch
15. wet hobo
16. porcine toupee
17. stupid finger
18. wheat-carrying vehicle
19. grass strength
20. inebriated animal

★ Inky Pinky ★

21. comical hare
22. vegetable for talking bird
23. unreliable dill
24. even demon
25. fishy operating room doctor
26. cross cat
27. gruesome tale
28. horrible couple
29. thin shaft
30. elementary skin eruption
31. indolent flower
32. strange stogie
33. drunk fortune-teller
34. strong-smelling tramp
35. basement resident
36. careful pupil
37. adroit finger-protector
38. small person's nervous habit
39. happy boat
40. doorway for guards
41. mob's chatter
42. threat on the court
43. light sprite
44. web-spinner's drink
45. nuptial land vehicle
46. superior woolen garment
47. simian textile trim
48. thrifty horn
49. herder of spotted cats
50. untippable piece of furniture

★ Inkity Pinkity ★

51. ominous clergyman
52. frozen bike
53. tantrum thrown by Cleopatra
54. pasta torn into little pieces
55. mundane pattern of tiles
56. cetacean's soundness of mind
57. conference about a head injury
58. pessimistic mountaintop
59. cluster of candy
60. horned animal's melon
61. how to save the environment
62. dead man's talk
63. elastic bushes
64. software contestor
65. Hebrew walking stick

Now it's time to step up to some prodigiously polysyllabic posers:

★ Inkitity Pinkitity ★

66. royal cloth
67. crazy leave of absence
68. floor-covering oil
69. maudlin Asian
70. self-reliant overseer
71. microscopic organisms in Russia
72. bubbly teenager
73. star war
74. deafening ancient chant
75. inoperative power plant

★ Inkititity Pinkititity ★

76. police lexicon

77. incapable scholar

78. meatless lover of
    things old

79. satisfaction from
    passing amendments

80. opinion article in
    tropical newspaper

Answers

Ink Pink: 1. cheap jeep 2. terse verse 3. weird beard 4. beef thief 5. big fig 6. vile smile 7. vault fault 8. dwarf wharf 9. wan swan 10. bright knight 11. daft raft 12. smart dart 13. trench stench 14. mean queen 15. damp tramp 16. pig wig 17. dumb thumb 18. grain train 19. lawn brawn 20. drunk skunk

Inky Pinky: 21. funny bunny 22. parrot carrot 23. fickle pickle 24. level devil 25. sturgeon surgeon 26. crabby tabby 27. gory story 28. gruesome twosome 29. narrow arrow 30. simple pimple 31. lazy daisy 32. bizarre cigar 33. tipsy gypsy 34. fragrant vagrant 35. cellar dweller 36. prudent student 37. nimble thimble 38. midget fidget 39. merry ferry 40. sentry entry 41. rabble babble 42. tennis menace 43. airy fairy 44. spider cider 45. marriage carriage 46. better sweater 47. gibbon ribbon 48. frugal bugle 49. leopard shepherd 50. stable table

Inkity Pinkity: 51. sinister minister 52. icicle bicycle 53. Egyptian conniption 54. spaghetti confetti 55. prosaic mosaic 56. manatee sanity 57. concussion discussion 58. cynical pinnacle 59. confection collection 60. antelope cantaloupe 61. pollution solution 62. cadaver palaver 63. rubbery shrubbery 64. computer disputer 65. Israeli shillelagh

Inkity Pinkity: 66. imperial material 67. fanatical sabbatical

68. linoleum petroleum 69. sentimental oriental 70. independent superintendent 71. Siberia bacteria 72. effervescent adolescent 73. constellation altercation 74. stentorian Gregorian 75. utility futility

Inkititity Pinkititity: 76. constabulary vocabulary 77. ineffectual intellectual 78. vegetarian antiquarian 79. ratification gratification 80. equatorial editorial

Making
the
Alphabet
Dance

Beyond our everyday use of language—"please pass the butter";"how much does that cost?"—gleams the world of wordplay:"I'd rather have a bottle in front of me than a frontal lobotomy";"What is the longest word in the English language? Smiles, because there's a 'mile' between the first and last letter."

A gorgeously blooming field of wordplay is letter play, and at the heart of letter play is the anagram, the rearranging of letters to uncover surprising relationships between words and phrases. There are more of us riding this planet than you think who tingle at the discovery that all the letters in the word conversation can be rearranged to form VOICES RANT ON and that southern California turns out to be HOT SUN, OR LIFE IN A CAR. Take it from me, Richard Lederer, who can now reveal himself as—ta! da!—RIDDLER REACHER.

Some of the books I've read about letter play are pretty much long, boring lists of examples; others are bouncy entertainments that don't teach their readers very much. In my work, I strive to present learning dressed up to have fun.

Ana Gram, the Juggler

Ladies and gentlemen and children of all ages!
Hurry! Hurry! Hurry!
Step right up and into a ring-a-ding circus of words!
Inside you'll ooh and aah at tremendous, stupendous, end-
over-endous
    words swinging from tent-tops!
    words teetering on tightropes!
    words swallowing swords and breathing fire!
    words jumping through flaming hoopla!
    words leaping onto the backs of galloping coursers!
    (all the while maintaining their equine-imity!)
    words thrusting their heads into the jaws of lions!
    bestial words—from Noah's aardvark to on beyond
        zebra!
    high-caliber words shot out of the canon of letter fun!
    words somersaulting, heels over head!
    words sporting and cavorting in billowy, pillowy clown
        suits!
    words pedaling their unisyllables!
    words perched high on stilts! midget words!
    elephantine word! toy poodle words!

sideshow words with shapes beyond the arean of ordinary life!

and letter-perfect words going for the juggler!

So, run don't walk, to the bar-none Barnum and Ballyhoo circus of words—the Palace in Wonderland that runs Ringlings around all others. Well, come to the sawdust stage of words, where all the humor is guaranteed to be in tents!

Can you create one word out of the letters in *new door*?

The answer is (ha ha) *one word*. The letters in *new door* are the same as those in *one word*, except in a different order.

When is enough not enough?

When you rearrange the letters in *enough*, you get *one hug*. Everybody knows that one hug is never enough!

These riddles involve anagrams. An anagram is a rearrangement of all the letters in a word, phrase, or name to form another word, phrase, or name.

To introduce you to the more spectacular examples of alphabetic manipulation, here is the greatest juggler in the world, the very art and soul of our circus of words—Ana Gram! She can twirl balls, clubs, plates, hoops, or flaming torches, but she's best when she's spinning letters. She starts with three letters, and when she really gets them going, she adds another and another and another and another and another and another, until the audience bursts into applause.

Ladies and Gentlemen! Boys and girls! Children of all ages! Don't *waddle*! Don't *dawdle*! It's time for Anagramarama! It's *tedious outside*, so stay inside and enjoy the fun *residing* at *ring-side*.

I give you a *genuine ingenue*, the high *priest* of *esprit* and *ripest sprite* of letter play of the highest *stripe*.

I *enlist* you to be *silent* and *listen* to the *inlets* of my *tinsel* words. As we *begin* our *binge* of letter juggling, *please* don't even think about falling *asleep*, or your *retina* will not *retain* the *overt trove* of *laudatory*, *adulatory* letter wizardry, which has for too long *continued unnoticed*.

Simple logic *impels* your positive *reactions* to Ana Gram's *creations*. Among *robust turbos*, she's an absolute *dynamo*, even on a *Monday*—a *gagster* who will *stagger* you with her *latent talent*. She's the *antagonist* of *stagnation*, the *flauntress* of *artfulness*, and the *patroness* of letter shuffling because she knows how to transmute a *sword* into *words*, which then *float aloft*. Each *emphatic*, *empathic seraph phrase*, each *snatch* of her *chants*, will *stanch* any trace of *mental lament* and *reclaim* the *miracle* of language.

For *various* reasons, Ana Gram is a *saviour* who *loves* to *solve* your woes and who *repeals* any *relapse*. Her *stagery gyrates* the *grayest* spirit. Before you *reunite* with your *retinue* or retreat through the *ingress*, please attend to this greatest of *singers*, a *singer* who *reigns* and will never *resign* as our *merriest rimester*. She's one of those crowd-*pleaser leapers* whose *dances ascend* to the *highest heights* as she performs a *toe dance* while relating an anecdote.

Ana Gram's *persistent prettiness* earns her *direct credit* for *regally* and *largely* curing any *allergy* in the *gallery*. No *dictionary* is *indicatory* of the *elation* you will experience down to your very *toenail*, a joy that will—from the *fringes* of your *fingers*, from your *elbow* to *below* the *bowel*, from your *bared beard* to your *viler liver* to your *venal navel*, from your *ears* to your *arse*, from the top of the *spine* to the tip of the *penis*—*roost* in the *roots* of your *torso*.

She is the very *heart* of the *earth*, a *damsel* who merits *medals*. With a *lovely volley* of letters, she juggles a *cheap peach*, an *Argentine tangerine*, and *solemn lemons* and *melons*. At the same time she *reaps*, *pares*, and then manages to *spear pears* while twirling *pastel plates* (a *staple* of her act) and balancing a *maraschino* on her nose and playing two *harmonicas*.

Pleased by what has *elapsed* and astounded by such *climaxes*, everyone *exclaims* that it would be impossible to *reproduce* her *procedure* to *intoxicate* your *excitation*. She never *mutilates*, but will only *stimulate ultimates*. She will not *enervate*, and you will *venerate*. She'll *edify*, and you will *deify* the *luster* of the *result* she'll unfailingly *rustle* up.

Lucky ladies and gentlemen! *Cripes!* Just think of the *prices* we offer, as advertised in *English* on the *shingle* that adorns our booth:

DISCOUNTER INTRODUCES REDUCTIONS

Look closely at the *poster*, and *presto!—boing! bingo!*— you'll see an *integral alerting, altering, relating triangle*. What we have here is a trianagram—three ten-letter words, each a re-arrangement of the other two! Now I, your circus pitchman, will be busy *mastering emigrants streaming* (a nine-letter triana-gram) into the tent. I hope that someone will have *cautioned* them not to have *auctioned* off their *education* (yet another nine-letter trianagram).

I, a *magnate gateman* who *patrols* these *portals* with your kind *permission*, have the *impression* that you brand me a *blab-bing, babbling funfair ruffian*, a *has-been banshee*, a *tearing in-grate, infield infidel*, and *errant ranter*. You may wish to *compile* a *polemic lamenting* my *alignment* as one of those *nameless sales-men* and *dishonest hedonists* who are full of *tangible bleating* and *impressing simperings*. You may claim that I who *ratchet* up the *chatter* with *supersonic percussion* am a *rowdy, wordy vice-dean* of *deviance*. You will be *eager* to *agree* that I'm a *trifling, flirting baritone obtainer* of *untidy nudity* who *seldom models* his *ideals* for *ladies*.

I may *madden* you and cause you to *demand* that I be *damned*, before you *depart*, convinced that I have *prated* and should be hoist on my own *petard*, *bombed* and *mobbed*. But any *unstirred intruders* and *outbred doubter* who may *obtrude* should come to the *realization* that people tend to *rationalize*. *Irately* and *tearily*, I tell you that, in *reality*, to be *portrayed* as one so *predatory* causes me *mental lament*. Anyone who accuses me of being a *usurping, pursuing, daemonic comedian* is simply being an *inconsistent nonscientist*.

Truth be told, I'm an *Einstein* of the *nineties—a gentleman, an elegant man* who gets *blamed* because I have *ambled* into *bed-lam*. It's one of the *noisier ironies*. *However, whoever* enters needs no *caveat* to *vacate* this *auction* with *caution*. I *certify* that

I will *rectify* the situation and *deposit* the *dopiest rowdies* and *weirdos* in the *closest closets*.

The *charisma* of Ana's performance *is a charm*, a *charm* that you see *march* before your eyes. In her, you *observe* the *obverse* of the very *verbose*. After the *mite* of an *item* that follows, I guarantee that at no *time* will you *emit groans* from your *organs*:

Arty Idol

Watch Ana Gram, and you will see
Her act inspires idolatry.
Please do not come o tardily,
And dilatory please don't be.

★

Adroitly Ana Gram will start
To alter daily rot. She's smart:
A dirty lot, an oily dart,
She'll change into the doily art.

An affinity of meaning often generates an infinity of pleasure. Our arty idol Ana Gram can whirl the word *Episcopal* and create both *a Popsicle* and *Pepsi-Cola*. She tosses up a *raptor* and down swoops a *parrot*. She can even transform *dyslexia* into DAILY SEX (is that a cause or a cure?) and *antidisestablishmentarianism* into I AM AN ARTIST, AND I BLESS THIS IN ME!

But it is even more fascinating to watch Ana reconfigure words and expressions into other words or statements that bear a meaningful relationship to the base. These significant tandems are called aptagrams—words that anagram into their own synonyms or to uncannily related ideas. You clearly possess *the sense of humor* and think, "OH, THERE'S SOME FUN!" So for your entertainment I present a parade of meaningful-phrase anagrams, the *athletics* of which are LITHE ACTS. Because they are so *appropriate*, they are absolutely A-I, APT, PROPER.

Ana Gram is *an acrobat*—ACT ON A BAR—as she juggles letters *alphabetically* and laughs, "I PLAY ALL THE ABC." So full of *endearments* is her magic that we bestow TENDER NAMES upon her.

You, dear *patron*, may want NO PART of me. Your *animosity* IS NO AMITY, I know. You may call me a *blatherskite* and think, THIS BE TALKER. *Ridiculous?* I LUDICROUS. That's *asinine*; it IS INANE. So don't be *mean-spirited* and IN A DISTEMPER. Remember that *villainousness* is AN EVIL SOUL'S SIN. So *bury the hatchet* and BUTCHER THY HATE.

Now that Ana Gram is *enshrined* in your memory, we'll SEND HER IN for a GRAND FINALE—A FLARING END. After *the eyes* THEY SEE and *this ear* IT HEARS her nimble *executions*, she EXITS ON CUE, and we exclaim in *unanimity*, "AM IN UNITY! *Mirabile dictu:* I DUB IT A MIRACLE!"

No wonder that an acronym of *anagram* is A New, Appropriate, Grandly Rearranged, Alphabetic Message. No wonder that those who believe in the magical potency of words have hailed *the anagram* as AH, AN ART GEM! and *anagrams* as ARS MAGNA, "the great art"!

Since 1926, the zoological magazine for my city, San Diego, has carried the title ZOONOOZ. I suspect that even back then the creators of the magazine knew that ZOONOOZ was a palindrome.

Even if you're a dud, kook, boob, or poop, you may know that in 1941, the name radar was coined to describe a radio device used to locate an object by means of waves reflected from the object and received by the sending unit. The letters in radar form not only an acronym ("radio detecting and ranging"), but an especially happy palindromic coinage for the two-way reflection of radio waves.

Alistair Reid expresses what may be at the heart of our fascination for matters palindromic: "The dream which occupies the tortuous mind of every palindromist is that somewhere within the confines of the language lurks the Great Palindrome, the nutshell which not only fulfills the intricate demands of the art, flowing sweetly in both directions, but which also contains The Final Truth of Things."

In the disquisition on palindromes you're about to read, I have another opportunity to do what I enjoy best— to embed the concept in the narrative, in this instance by means of a camel for whom I would walk a mile.

The Palindromedary

Back in 1907, one A. C. Pearson asked readers to identify the word described in his little poem:

> A *turning point in every day,*
> *Reversed I do not alter.*
> *One half of me says haste away!*
> *The other bids me falter.*

The answer is *noon*. Half the word is *on* ("haste away!"), and half is *no* ("bids me falter"). Together they form a word that reads the same forwards and backwards.

A palindrome is a word, a *word row*, a sentence, or a longer statement that communicates the same message when the letters of which it is composed are read in reverse order. Palindromes make us exult, *Ah ha!*, *Oh, ho!*, *Hey, yeh!*, *Yo boy!*, *Yay!*, *Wow!*, *Tut-tut!*, *Har-har! Rah-rah!*, *Heh-heh!*, and *Hoorah! Har! Ooh!* and *Ahem! It's time. Ha!*

Palindromic words are *summus*, palindromic Latin for "the highest, uppermost, the top." But it is to the sentence palindrome that we must turn to discover the most celebrated and adroit exercises in palindromic power and potentiality. Some

logolepts claim that the first sentence ever spoken was a palindrome. We are told that the Deity plunged Adam into a deep
sleep prior to extracting a rib wherewith to make him a help-
meet. When he awoke, Adam to his amazement found Eve
(possessing the first palindromic name, of course) by his side.
Having no one to introduce him, he politely bowed and said:
MADAM, I'M ADAM.

Name Me Man

Backward and forward, as you will perceive,
Read Adam's first greeting to dear Mother Eve:
MADAM, I'M ADAM. Now we can conceive
That her answer was simply: EVE, MAD ADAM, EVE.

Another famous palindromic sentence was purportedly uttered by Napoleon (in English, of course—so convenient) as he
paced the shores of Elba in 1814—ABLE WAS I ERE I SAW ELBA:

Elba Fable

ABLE WAS I ERE I SAW ELBA,
Napoleon cried like a toy-deprived kid.
Wellington mocked in reply, DID I
DISABLE ELBA'S ID? I DID.

The third, and newest, in the triumvirate of best-known
palindromes describes the saga of George Washington
Goethals: A MAN! A PLAN! A CANAL! PANAMA!:

Route Canal

There was a man who had a plan.
It wasn't banal to build a canal.
His critics tried to ban him, pan him. Ah!
A MAN! A PLAN! A CANAL! PANAMA!

One of the oldest palindromes appears as a legend on several fountains in Europe, including St. Sophia in Constantinople, Notre Dame in Paris, and St. Martin's in London. The Greek message reads, NIΨON ANOMHMA, MH MONAN OΨIN: "Wash your sins, not only your face."

The first recorded sentence palindrome in English comes from the hand of the early seventeenth-century poet John Taylor: LEWD DID I LIVE & EVIL I DID DWEL. *Dwel* is acceptable seventeenth-century spelling, but the ampersand is a bit of a fudge factor. Still, Taylor's nine-word effort is a promising palindromic path-breaker for the two-way extravaganzas in our circus of words.

Ladies and gentlemen! Children of all ages! We now present an exclusive interview with the Palindromedary himself, the two-way statement made flesh. This camel is a talking animal smitten with ailihphilia—the love of palindromes. Thus, whenever the Palindromedary makes a statement, that sentence, SIDES REVERSED, IS the very same sentence.

BARKER: So you're the famous Palindromedary?

PALINDROMEDARY: I, MALE, MACHO, OH, CAMEL AM I.

I see that, despite your fame, you're wearing a name tag. Why?

GATEMAN SEES NAME. GARAGEMAN SEES NAME TAG.

Is it true that people will walk a mile to see your act?

OK, SAY A MILE, MAC. A CAMEL I MAY ASK, O.

Is it true that you were discovered in the Nile region?

CAMEL IN NILE, MAC.

How are you able to speak entirely in palindromes?

SPOT WORD ROW. TOPS!

What kind of word row?

WORD ROW? YA, WOW! TWO-WAY WORD ROW.

I understand that when you insert SIDES REVERSED IS into the middle of a palindrome, it becomes more than twice as long. Please offer an example.

"WORD ROW? YA, WOW! TWO-WAY WORD ROW" SIDES RE-VERSED IS "WORD ROW? YA, WOW! TWO-WAY WORD ROW."

Let's talk about the Word Circus animal acts. I heard that the trainer said an earful to the flying elephant in your menagerie. What was the trainer's command?

"DUMBO, LOB MUD."

I hear Dan, the lion tamer, is sick in bed and won't get up.

POOR DAN IS IN A DROOP.

Would it cheer Dan up if we dressed him in a colorful outfit?

MIRTH, SIR, A GAY ASSET? NO, DON'T ESSAY A GARISH TRIM.

So there won't be a lion performance today?

NO, SIT! CAT ACT IS ON.

Have you seen the big cats perform?

OH WHO WAS IT I SAW, OH WHO?

Well, have you seen the big cats in action?

WAS IT A CAR OR A CAT I SAW?

In addition to the big cat act, will we be witnessing performing dogs?

A DOG? A PANIC IN A PAGODA!

If we're not going to see a dog act, where are the dogs kept?

POOCH COOP.

I heard that somebody slipped something into the dog cage.

GOD! A RED NUGGET! A FAT EGG UNDER A DOG!

How did the dog take the prank?

HE GODDAMN MAD DOG, EH.

What happened when you followed the dog act?

DID I STEP ON DOG DOO? GOOD GOD! NO PETS! I DID!

Why aren't the owls performing tonight?

TOO HOT TO HOOT.

And the panda?

PANDA HAD NAP.

And the elk?

ELK CACKLE.

But where are the deer?

DEER FRISK, SIR, FREED.

I hear that the animals each get into a cart and have a race around the ring.

TIED, I RIDE IT.

Did you participate in the last animal race?

NO. WE NOT RACE. CART ONE WON.

I understand that the menagerie also includes gnus and zebras.

O GNU, FAR BE ZEBRA FUN! GO!

And did the gnus actually sing the "Star Spangled Banner"?

RISE, NUT! GNUS SUNG TUNE, SIR.

Did the rats join them?

RATS GNASH TEETH; SANG STAR.

What about the rumor that one of the gnus is ill?

UNGASTROPERITONITIS: "IS IT I? NOT I," REPORTS A GNU.

What's the problem when you come after the gnu act?

GNU DUNG.

Will we see a yak?

KAY, A RED NUDE, PEEPED UNDER A YAK.

Is it true that Kay rode on your back rather than taking a taxi cab?

HA, BAREBACK RIDER'S RED! IRK CAB ERA, BAH!

Is it also true that you sewed a dress for the kangaroo?

I MADE KANGAROO TUTU. TOO RAG-NAKED AM I.

Speaking of kangaroos, what's your advice on how to train a young wallaby?

LAY A WALLABY BABY BALL AWAY, AL.

What's one of your favorite human circus acts?

TRAPEZE PART.

And what's especially exciting about the trapeze?

TEN ON TRAPEZE PART! NO NET!

No net?

NO TENT NET ON.

Shall we identify and summon the acrobats to perform with the trapeze artists?

TAB OR CALL ACROBAT.

And how do the acrobats train children for their act?

PUPILS ROLL A BALL OR SLIP UP.

I've heard that you occasionally have problems with warts and that you rub your straw on those warts to gain relief.

STRAW? NO! TOO STUPID A FAD. I PUT SOOT ON WARTS.

Have you ever tried fasting to lose weight?

DOC, NOTE. I DISSENT. A FAST NEVER PREVENTS A FATNESS. I DIET ON COD.

So what food do you like to eat the most—salami or lasagna?

GO HANG A SALAMI. I'M A LASAGNA HOG.

So what did you emphasize in your diet?

DESSERTS I STRESSED.

Desserts were at the center of your diet?

I SAW DESSERTS. I'D NO LEMONS, ALAS, NO MELON; DIS-TRESSED WAS I.

Why do you have a no-smoking policy at the Word Circus?

CIGAR? TOSS IT IN A CAN. IT IS SO TRAGIC.

So every single cigar and cigarette have been thrown out?

NO TRACE. NOT ONE CARTON.

Not one?

BUT SAD EVA SAVED A STUB.

Eva?

EVA CAN, IN A CAVE.

Can you point out Eva for us?

EVA, WE'RE HERE. WAVE.

You seem truly excited about the circus of words.

AVID AS A DIVA.

Are there any acts that you would get rid of?

DUDE, NOT ONE DUD.

But what do you say to those who contend that the circus can't survive as an art form?

NO! IT CAN! ACTION!

Can the corporate world save the circus?

NO, IT IS OPPOSED. ART SEES TRADE'S OPPOSITION.

So the business world is not for you?

NO, IT'S A BOZO BASTION.

Will the circus of words continue to evolve?

ARE WE NOT DRAWN ONWARD, WE FEW, DRAWN ONWARD TO NEW ERA?

Mr. Palindromedary, we thank you for such a scintillating two-way interview. Is it true that you are the only animal who can speak intelligibly in palindromes?

YES, THAT'S TRUE. ALL OTHER ANIMALS SAY THINGS LIKE, "EKILS GNIH TYASS LAMINAR EHTOLLAE URTSTAHT SEY."

Once upon a time, when the sky was made of canvas and the ground was made of sawdust, elephants in tutus danced on their toes and cradled showgirls in their trunks.

Once upon a time, fountains of red hair spouted from high white foreheads, and saggy, baggy clowns spilled into our laughter.

Once upon a time, when we were young and full of wonder, acrobats in spangled tights flew through the air like birds, and plumed horses pranced to the music of steam calliopes.

Once upon a time, there was magic in our land, and that magic was the circus.

That magic has lived on in my heart and imagination, and many of my poems about language I have cast in circus imagery.

A Circus of Poems

From alpha to omega,
You can bet the alphabet,
Like a painting done by Degas,
Will leap and pirouette.

★

See dancing words, entrancing words,
Sterling words unfurling.
Watch prancing words, enhancing words,
Whirling, twirling, swirling.

Let's hop right on the bandwagon and face the music of our language. I don't wish to chime in on your life and harp on the subject. I just want to pull out all the stops and strike a responsive chord in you. May the following be music to your ears:

The Bandwagon

Now the tent grows dark, and the crowd grows hush.
Then the spotlight shines, and the space grows lush
With the cymbals' clash and the tinkled heat,
The triangle's ting and the snare drum's beat,
As our hungry hearts and the empty air
Fill to the brim with a brassy blare.

★

Our jaws a-droop and our eyes a-light
And our cheeks ablaze at the gorgeous sight:
All golden and crimson and purple and blue—
A calliope dream that we never knew:
With the chest-deep pulse of the kettledrums,
Into the ring the bandwagon comes.

★

Then the wha-wha-wha of the slide trombone,
And the pitter-boink-boink of the xylophone,
And the umpa umpa umpa umps
Of tubas kissed by men with mumps,
And the twang and the wang and the whacka whacka whack
Of banjo wheels on a circus track.

★

Ah, the rattle and rhyme of the music's time
Brim our hungry hearts with a song sublime!

Now hear the music of some letter-perfect verse, with many words composed entirely of letter sounds. Keep in mind that the same letter twice in a row sounds like a plural. For example, II means "eyes."

	TRANSLATION
YURYY	*Why you are wise*
Is EZ to C	*Is easy to see.*
U should B called	*You should be called*
"XLNC."	*"Excellency."*
U XEd NE	*You exceed any*
MT TT.	*Empty tease.*
I NV how U	*I envy how you*
XL with EE.	*Excel with ease.*

What do you call a naked grizzly? A bare bear. And what do you call a pony with a sore throat? A hoarse horse. Homo-

phones are clusters of words that are each spelled differently
but that sound exactly the same.

Hears a rye peace eye maid up inn my idol thyme. Aye rote
it four yew two sea Howe homophones Cannes seam sew whiled
from there knows write too they're tows. With pried, eye no it
will knot boar ewe. Its meant two bee red allowed:

A Bazaar Tail
*One **night** a **knight** on a **hoarse horse***
***Rode** out upon a **road**.*
*This **male wore mail** for **war** and **would***
*Explore a **wood** that glowed.*

*His **tale** I'll tell from head to **tail**.*
*I'll **write** his **rite** up **right**.*
*A hidden **site** our hero found,*
*A **sight** that I shall **cite**.*

*With **woe** he shouted, **"Whoa!"** as **rain***
*Without a **break** did **reign**.*
*To **brake**, he pulled the **rein**, and like*
*A shattered **pane**, felt **pain**.*

*The poor knight met a **witch, which** made*
*Sweat **pour** from every **pore**.*
*He'd never **seen** a **scene** like that.*
*His **sore** heart couldn't **soar**.*

Then they a game for truffles played,
In which he **mined** her **mind.**
To prove who was the **better bettor**
And **find** who should be **fined.**

★

He **won one** twice, he won **two, too.**
To **grate** on her felt **great.**
To **wrest** the **rest,** he went **for four,**
And, at the **fore, ate eight.**

★

Due to her loss, the **mourning** witch,
'Midst **morning mist** and **dew,**
Her truffles **missed. I know no way,**
Do I, to **weigh** her rue.

★

Our knight began to **reel, for real.**
The **world whirled,** so to speak.
All the **days** of the **week** his **sole soul** felt
The dizzy **daze** of the **weak.**

★

Our **heir** to knighthood gave it up.
He felt the **fare** not **fair.**
His **wholly holy sword soared** up
As he **threw** it **through** the air.

★

The bell has **tolled,** I'm **told.** The **hour**
To end **our** tale draws nigh.
Without **ado,** I bid **adieu,**
So **by** your leave, **bye-bye.**

Often, the more demanding the restrictions, the more fun I have making a poem. I had an exhilarating time writing this little ditty, in which each of the eleven lines is composed of just the six letters in the name Daniel:

> *An idle*
> *Lead-in*
> *Ad line:*
> *DANIEL,*
> *Nailed*
> *In deal*
> *(i.e., land*
> *In dale),*
> *Led in a*
> *Denial*
> *And lie.*

In letter play, beheadment is the lopping off of the initial letters of a word. Gaze in wonder as, one at a time, the letters in *prelate* disappear from the front of the word:

> *The **prelate** did **relate** a tale*
> *Meant to **elate** both you and me.*
> *We stayed up **late** and **ate** our meal,*
> *"**Te** Deum" sang in key of **e**.*

Ladies and gentlemen! Boys and Girls! Wordsters of all ages! Our circus is no dog-and-pony show—and to prove it, please turn your attention to the hippodrome track engirding the sawdust

rings. Forget all the hype and hoopla, and fix your eyeballs upon
the greatest cavalcade of animals ever brought together!:

Paraders of the Lost Aardvark

All of Solomon's processions
And Croesus' gold and Trump's possessions
Cannot rival half the pomp
Of animals that march and romp.

★

What soul among us does not thrill
To a fiery hoop and a lion's skill,
The chittering of a monkey's laugh,
The mottled grace of a slim giraffe?

★

Who can be deaf to the ponderous sound
Of pachyderms that shake the ground,
Leathery monarchs lifting high
Their trumpet trunks to canvas sky?

★

Who is so proud as not to feel
'A secret awe before a seal
That keeps such slick and moist repose
Spinning a ball upon its nose?

★

Who can forget a mighty horse
Capering through its circle course?
Who is so old who fails to heed
A lady in pink on a milk-white steed?

Being a marsupial, a mother kangaroo carries her young in her pouch. Kangaroo words do the same thing: Within their letters they conceal a smaller version of themselves—a joey, which is what a kangaroo's offspring is called. The joey must be the same part of speech as the mother kangaroo, and its letters must appear in the same order.

The special challenge of kangaroo words is that the joey must be a synonym; it must have the same meaning as the fully grown word. A *plagiarist* is a kind of *liar*. On the job, your *supervisor* is your *superior*. I tried to summon as many kangaroo words as I could to hop through this poem:

Ab-Original Words

Hop right up to those kangaroo words,
Slyly concealing whiz-bangaroo words,
Accurate *synonyms,* **cute** *and* **acute,**
Hidden **diminutive** *words, so* **minute.**

*

Lurking inside of **myself** *you'll find* **me.**
Just as inside of **himself** *you'll find* **he.**
Feel your mind **blossom;** *feel your mind* **bloom:**
Inside a **catacomb's** *buried a* **tomb.**

*

Kangaroo words are **precocious** *and* **precious,**
Flourishing, lush *words that truly refresh us.*
We're **nourished;** *they* **nurse, elevate,** *and* **elate** *us.*
We're so **satisfied** *when their synonyms* **sate** *us.*

*

*Kangaroo words both **astound** us and **stun**.*
*They're so darned **secure** that we're **sure** to have fun!*
*With **charisma** and **charm**, they're a letter-play wonder.*
*They **dazzle** and **daze** with their treasures, down under.*

Here follows my favorite animal procession. I was inspired by Dr. William Archibald Spooner, who gave us so many wonderful tips of the slung—oops: slips of the tongue. Through his tang-tongueled whiz and witdom, the famous Oxford professor has bequeathed our language the word *spoonerism*, meaning a humorous reversal of consonant or vowel sounds:

Dr. Spooner's Animal Act
Welcome, ladies; welcome gents.
Here's an act that's so in tents:
An absolute surefire parade,
A positive pure-fire charade—
With animals weak and animals mild,
Creatures meek and creatures wild,
With animals all in a row.
We hope that you enjoy the show:

★

Gallops forth a curried horse,
Trotting through a hurried course.
Ridden by a loving shepherd
Trying to tame a shoving leopard.

Don't think I'm a punny phony,
But next in line's a funny pony.
On its back a leaping wizard,
Dancing with a weeping lizard.

★

Watch how that same speeding rider
Holds aloft a reading spider.
Now you see a butterfly
Bright and nimbly flutter by,
Followed by a dragonfly,
As it drains its flagon dry.
Step right up; see this mere bug
Drain the drink from his beer mug.

★

Lumbers forth a honey bear,
Fur as soft as bunny hair.
Gaze upon that churning bear,
Standing on a burning chair.
Gently patting a mute kitten,
On each paw a knitted mitten.
Watch as that small, running cat
Pounces on a cunning rat.

★

See a clever, heeding rabbit
Who's acquired a reading habit,
Sitting on his money bags,
Reading many bunny mags,

Which tickle hard his funny bone,
As he talks on his bunny phone.
He is such a funny beast,
Gobbling down his bunny feast.

★

Gasp in awe as winking seals
Sit atop three sinking wheels.
Don't vacillate. An ocelot
Will oscillate a vase a lot.
There's a clever dangling monkey
And a stubborn, mangling donkey
And—a gift from our Dame Luck—
There waddles in a large lame duck.

★

That's Dr. Spooner's circus show.
With animals all in a row,
(As you can see, we give free reign
To this metrical refrain.)
Now hops a dilly of a frog
Followed by a frilly dog.
Hear that hoppy frog advise:
"Time's fun when you're having flies!"

Life is a circus where thousands throng but none can stay. The only permanence of the circus is its impermanence. Each time the Greatest Show on Earth leaves a city, it tears itself down and piles itself onto railroad cars. Not so with the Word Circus.

Nothing now to mark the spot
But a littered vacant lot.
Sawdust in a heap, and where
The center ring stood, grass worn bare.

★

But remains the alphabet,
Ready to leap and pirouette.
May the spangled letters soar
In your head forevermore.

May all your days be circuses.